T0209350

ALSO BY GABRIEL O. AKINBODE

*God at Work: A Short History of the Fellowship of
Evangelical Groups in the Western Part of MCN*
(Ibadan: Scripture Union Press, 1992)

Marvelous in Our Eyes (Ibadan: Feyisetan Press, 1998)

*Christ's Gift of Congregational Life in the Ministry of Holy
Communion:* A professional project submitted to the Theological
School of Drew University in partial fulfillment of the
requirements for the Doctor of Ministry degree (2013)

The Neglected Great Commission

EVANGELISM

Gabriel O. Akinbode

WESTBOW
PRESS®
A DIVISION OF THOMAS NELSON
& ZONDERVAN

This book is a work of non-fiction. Unless otherwise noted, the author and the publisher make no explicit guarantees as to the accuracy of the information contained in this book and in some cases, names of people and places have been altered to protect their privacy.

WestBow Press books may be ordered through booksellers or by contacting:

WestBow Press
A Division of Thomas Nelson & Zondervan
1663 Liberty Drive
Bloomington, IN 47403
www.westbowpress.com
844-714-3454

Unless otherwise indicated, scripture quotations are taken from the New King James Version. Copyright © 1982 by Thomas Nelson, Inc. Used by permission. All rights reserved.

Scripture quotations marked KJV are taken from the Holy Bible, King James Version.

Scripture quotations marked NIV are taken from the Holy Bible, New International Version®, NIV®. Copyright © 1973, 1978, 1984 by Biblica, Inc.™ Used by permission of Zondervan. All rights reserved worldwide.

ISBN: 979-8-3850-0519-2 (sc)
ISBN: 979-8-3850-0608-3 (hc)
ISBN: 979-8-3850-0518-5 (e)

Library of Congress Control Number: 2023915172

Print information available on the last page.

WestBow Press rev. date: 08/25/2023

For the Methodist Evangelical Movement's (MEM) Golden Jubilee Celebration, Agodi Diocese of Methodist Church, Nigeria, and the Brooklyn Southwest Cooperative Parish of Long Island, West District, New York Conference of the United Methodist Church, United States.

CONTENTS

INTRODUCTION

This book, *The Neglected Great Commission: Evangelism*, is an American remembrance of *Marvelous in Our Eyes*, a book I published to celebrate the silver jubilee of the Methodist Evangelical Movement (MEM) in the Methodist Church, Nigeria, in 1998. This year, 2023, marks the golden jubilee of the Methodist Evangelical Movement, and it behooves me to reiterate the revolution we started as young people, bringing back the glory of evangelism to all Methodist churches and other denominations in Nigeria and beyond, as established by John Wesley.

Around that time, a prophecy came forth during one of our fellowships. It said that some people among us would be scattered to various parts of the world by God to lift up the Gospel. Little did I know then that my family and I would be relocated to the United States. Some of our fervent brothers and sisters are currently scattered in various parts of the world to serve the Lord!

In 2000, I was serving as pastor at Bodija Methodist Church in Ibadan, Nigeria. One of my church members gave me a United States visa lottery form. It was strange to me because I had never thought about doing it before, but I prayerfully filled in the form. Not quite long after she mailed it for me, another person at my job at the Oyo State Agricultural Development Program gave me another form, which I likewise filled out and mailed. As if those were not enough for confirmation, the boss of my wife at her place of work in the Ibadan Secretariat was going to give her another form, but she told her boss that her husband had mailed some out. To my amazement, in April 2001, I received a package in the mail that I had been successful out of the millions of people who had applied. That was how I got to the United States in February 2002, and my family joined me in June of the same year.

I give much thanks to Venerable Samuel Jegede and his family for helping my family and me a lot by ensuring a seamless transition to and settlement in the United States. Venerable Samuel Biodun Jegede was also a member of the Methodist Evangelical Movement in Nigeria before he relocated to the United States, which brought us closer together. While we were with them, we always went to their church—Christ Life Ministries Inc.—in Brooklyn, New York, which was led by Bishop Julius and Matilda Abiola. We enjoyed Bishop Abiola's hospitality.

After settling down, I went to the Theological School, Drew University, where I obtained my Master of Divinity degree and doctorate in the areas of worship, preaching, and spirituality. I became an ordained elder in the New York Annual Conference of the United Methodist Church and subsequently served as pastor for Cuyler-Warren United Methodist Church in Brooklyn, for four years, Immanuel and First Spanish United Methodist Church in Brooklyn for three years, Bloomfield United Methodist Church in Bloomfield, Connecticut, for four years, Red Hook United Methodist Church in Red Hook, New York, for two years, and

Christ United Methodist Church in Brooklyn for seven years. I am currently serving as the coordinator of Brooklyn Southwest Cooperative Parish, which has six churches, including Christ United Methodist Church in Brooklyn, and seven pastors.

Since my years in the ministry, I have been humbly used by God in the areas of revival services, Bible teachings, deliverance ministrations, and Christian leadership. I have served in various capacities in the Ministries of Methodist Church in Nigeria, including as the president of the Evangelical Group of Agodi Methodist Church, the coordinator of the Evangelical Movement in Ibadan Diocese, the president of Combined Evangelical Groups in the Western Zone of Nigeria, and the Bible study coordinator, assistant secretary, and eventually general secretary of the National Methodist Evangelical Movement. I served as the pastor of Agugu Methodist Church, in Ibadan, Nigeria, for three years and Bodija Methodist Church in Ibadan for three years as a non-stipendiary tent-making pastor before coming to the United States in 2002. As chairperson of the Bible Study Committee, I wrote most of the Bible study series used by the Evangelical groups and the Methodist Evangelical Movement in Nigeria.

In the United States, I crafted seventy-five Bible study outlines for Cuyler-Warren United Methodist Church in Brooklyn, many of which were also used for Immanuel and First Spanish United Methodist Church in Brooklyn and other churches where I served. I authored *God at Work: A Short History of the Fellowship of Evangelical Groups in the Western Part of MCN* (Ibadan: Scripture Union Press, 1992) and *Marvelous in Our Eyes* (Ibadan: Feyisetan Press, 1998).

I was a board member of the Division of Bloomfield Adult Education from 2011 to 2014 and a board member of the Theological School Alumni Association, Drew University, New Jersey, from 2013 to 2020. Since 2020, I have been a board member of Anchor House, a faith-based intensive residential treatment program licensed by OASAS in Brooklyn.

My wife, Grace, and my children, Eri, Ewa, and Ebun, are collaborators with me in the ministry, and I always render accordion music with my wife during ministrations.

Having humbly made an introduction of myself and my experiences, I must now discuss the Christian life. Firstly, anyone who wants to live the Christian life must understand that this life is a journey with an important beginning: salvation. I began this journey when I consciously surrendered my life to Jesus Christ as my Lord and Savior on Saturday, January 16, 1971. On that glorious Saturday, I had just resumed at Ibadan Grammar School, Molete, Ibadan, Nigeria, as a new student. I was staying in the boardinghouse.

As I went to the nearby tank to draw water, one of the students approached me and invited me to the chapel for the Scripture Union Fellowship that would start at 6:00 p.m. Being a churchgoer in my church, I gladly accepted the invitation and went. The fellowship was very lively and was filled with spiritual songs. At the time of ministration in the Word of God, an invited guest from the Christian Union at the University of Ibadan went to the podium and started preaching about how "you must be born again." The scripture he used was John 3:1–7. In his exposition, he narrated the life of Nicodemus and emphasized that if such an important personality as Nicodemus could come to Jesus, nothing should hinder us from doing the same. Before he finished the message, the Holy Spirit had given me conviction, and when the altar call was pronounced, I moved forward and surrendered to the Lord. Since that moment, I have been enjoying the presence of the Lord in my life. I had a rapid spiritual growth as I continued to fellowship with other believers. And since that time, the Lord has been using me for His glory.

What does it really mean to be saved? Many people are confused about this step and consequently make a lot of mistakes. One must know that salvation is not a result of trying to do good work, struggling to live a good life, or trying to pray well. Knowing the Bible verses very well and having the ability to preach good messages does not equate to being saved. Attending church regularly and being in the choir does not mean you are saved. Being baptized, being confirmed, and taking Holy Communion does not earn you salvation. The question might then become: "If by doing all this, one is not saved, what can one do to be saved?"

Here is the thing: Salvation is a result of encountering a *person*. That person is Jesus Christ, the Son of God, the Redeemer of the whole world. Salvation is a result of accepting Him personally as your Lord and Savior and inviting Him into your heart. It is an experiential occurrence. For salvation to take its effect, you must confess Jesus Christ as your personal Lord and Savior—repenting and forsaking your sins. You need to "confess with your mouth" and "believe in your heart that God has raised Him from the dead" (Rom. 10:9–10). When you have Jesus in your heart, you are saved. When you have Jesus in your heart, you become a child of God. When you have Jesus in your heart, He gives you the power to live above sin and please God. This is the foundation of what this book is all about.

I want to be clear to you, my reader, that there are some things you need to understand. First, know that you are a sinner and acknowledge it as the scripture says: "There is none righteous, no, not one … for all have sinned and fall short of the glory of God" (Rom. 3:10, 23).

Second, know that all sinners are doomed to die and be eternally separated from God: "For the wages of sin is death" (Rom. 6:23a).

Third, understand that you cannot save yourself from sin. You do not have that power—and no one else can do it for another or for themselves:

> For I know that in me (that is, in my flesh) nothing good dwells; for to will is present with me, but how to perform what is good I do not find. (Rom. 7:18)

> O wretched man that I am! Who will deliver me from this body of death? (Rom. 7:24)

> Nor is there salvation in any other, for there is no other name under heaven given among men by which we must be saved. (Acts 4:12)

Fourth, know that God loves you and has provided the solution for you through the Savior, Jesus Christ:

> For God so loved the world that He gave His only begotten Son, that whoever believes in Him should not perish but have everlasting life. (Jn. 3:16)

Fifth, believe in Jesus Christ. He has paid the penalty of sin and death for you on the cross at Calvary by dying your death and offering you eternal life.

Sixth, break yourself loose in the presence of God and penitently go into prayer, confessing your sins and asking for forgiveness. Ask Him to wash away your sins and cleanse you completely from all faults. Consciously tell Him to save you—and that you accept Him as your Lord and Savior from this moment. Promise Him that you will not go back and that He should give you the grace to continue with Him. Since you have sincerely come to Him, He will never forsake you no matter how heavy your sins have been:

> All that the Father gives Me will come to Me, and the one who comes to Me I will by no means cast out. (Jn. 6:37)

Believe that He has saved you and begin to thank Him, rejoicing that you have been saved and counted among the children of God.

I want to assure you that salvation is not dependent on your feelings or emotions. Salvation is based on the facts that are evident in the Bible. Salvation is by grace, through faith; it is an unmerited favor:

> Now faith is the substance of things hoped for, the evidence of things not seen. (Heb. 11:1)

Even after you have taken all the steps above, there is a tendency to still have persistent doubts about your salvation. You need to be studying the Bible. Every part of the Bible is the infallible Word of God, but you can begin to study from the Gospel of John to quickly gain the words of assurance. Better still, you can make use of a study guide such as "Daily Power," "Upper Room," or "Our Daily Bread." These guides will lead you to different parts of the Bible that will build up in you the assurance of your salvation, the assurance of the scriptures, the assurance of the indwelling Holy Spirit, the assurance of changes that have taken place in your life, the assurance of God's love to you, the assurance of victory you have received through the atoning blood of Jesus, the assurance of deliverance from the power of darkness, and the assurance of God's provision for your life.

When you are grounded in the Word of God, no matter what your circumstance may be, you will stand firm in the Lord. No matter what feelings are flashing through your mind, the Holy Spirit will continue to help you become strong in faith. You can be sure that the Holy Spirit "bears witness" with your "spirit" that you are a child of God (Rom. 8:16). He will fill your heart with great peace, serenity, and joy. All fears of guilt and doubts will disappear, and you can confidently confess your past errors and testify to how Christ has delivered you.

The Holy Spirit will help you grow daily to be like Jesus. There is so much that the Holy Spirit will help you achieve, and you will no longer struggle to live. He will equip you with understanding and love for the Word of God. Studying the Word of God will no longer be burdensome to you because the hunger to know more will be aroused in you all the time.

The Holy Spirit will give you the hunger for God, and the closer to God you are, the more hatred for sin you will have. Because the love of Christ has been poured into your heart, the urge to pray will always be in you. You will love to intercede for others for their salvation and for meeting their needs. You will also love to commit your ways into the hands of the Lord. You will also love to have fellowship with other Christians and share the love of Christ with the unsaved.

As a new convert, you will experience a new life. The sinful things you were doing before will no longer be convenient for you. There will be a great change once you are born again!

> Therefore, if anyone is in Christ, he is a new creation; old things have passed away; behold, all things have become new. (2 Cor. 5:17)

There will be a great change of standards and values. You will feel uncomfortable with all fashion and ways of life that are not pleasing to God. Old friends whose way of life caused you to sin will not be of interest to you anymore except those who are ready to turn to Christ. Because of the love you have for them, you will make all the efforts for them to know Christ, but if they refuse to yield, you will be careful to avoid committing sin with them. In short, you will be more inclined to stand up for Jesus than to compromise with the world. Of course, that will not make you reduce your love for them. As Christ loves everybody, you will continue to show love to them, but you will avoid following their sinful lives.

1

THE ETYMOLOGICAL
MEANING OF EVANGELISM

1.1 The Etymological Meaning of Evangelism

The etymology of *evangelism* derives from the Greek verb *euangelizomai*, which means "to bring or announce good news." And the Greek from which we get our word *Gospel, euangelion*, simply means "good news." It is only natural then that evangelism should come to be heavily associated with announcing and proclaiming the Gospel. Both Western Evangelical and Eastern Orthodox Christians have—for the most part—favored this view of evangelism.

Thus, the Lausanne covenant[1] says that to evangelize is to spread the good news that Jesus Christ died for our sins and was raised from the dead according to the scriptures. As the reigning Lord, He now offers the forgiveness of sins and the liberating gift of the Holy Spirit to all who repent and believe.

---

[1] J. Stott, *The Lausanne Covenant. Exposition and Commentary* (Minneapolis: World Wide Publication, 1975), 20.

In the eighteenth century, no one would have thought of referring to John Wesley or George Whitefield as evangelists. In the nineteenth century, similar pastors would have been known in most quarters as "revivalists," the common designation for itinerant preachers.[2] In fact, evangelism, like its conceptual cousin, *evangelization*, only came into prominence in the late nineteenth century. For arbitrary reasons, the latter term got lost and has now surfaced in ecumenical circles as an alternative to evangelism. Somehow, there is less stigma attached to the term *evangelization*—even though usage since the late nineteenth century makes it virtually impossible to separate them in meaning. Of course, one can always discern a difference in meaning between them, but the fact remains that historically the two terms have been similar.

The prevailing conception of evangelism in Western Christianity is tied intimately to the proclamation of the Christian Gospel. Most Christians, if asked to define *evangelism*, would naturally construe it as announcing, communicating, or proclaiming the Christian message to those outside the Christian faith. Dictionary definitions from both Britain and North America support this. *Webster's Third International Dictionary*[3] defines *evangelism* as "the proclamation of the Gospel; especially the presentation of the Gospel to individuals by such methods as preaching, teaching, and personal or visitation

---

[2] A. C. Krass, *Applied Theology 1*: "Go and make Disciples" Pub. In Association with the United Society for Christian Litt. For the Theological Education Fund, London, SPCK.

[3] *Webster's Third International Dictionary.*

programs." In the *Oxford English Dictionary,*[4] *evangelism* is "the preaching or promulgation of the Gospel." Likewise, an *evangelist* is defined as an itinerant preacher who proclaims the Christian message wherever he or she will receive a hearing.

Evangelization is defined as the action or word of preaching the Gospel. Other sources refer to "instructing in the Gospel," "bringing under the influence of the Gospel," and the like. However, the prevailing impression is that evangelism is basically the preaching of the Christian message to those who will hear. And this is understood by the conventional image of the evangelist as an itinerant Christian worker who preaches the Gospel and calls people to commitment to Jesus Christ as Savior and Lord.

The Greek verb *kerussein,* which translates to "preach" in English, means to "proclaim" or "announce." This verb comes from the noun *kerux,* which means a herald. A herald is one who goes before a king or a chief to announce that he is coming, goes in the direction of a king or chief to announce his will, or gives his instructions, edict, or laws.

As heralds of Christ, the message that we are to announce is the *evangel.* The word *evangel* comes from the Greek word *euangelion,* which means "good news." *Angelion* means "news," and *eu* means "good" (the good news concerning Jesus Christ). By God's order, we preachers are to tell all people what He has done in Jesus Christ. Through us who are His messengers in all parts of the world, we—Americans, Africans, Europeans, Asians, Koreans, Indians, Nigerians, Kenyans, et cetera—are to learn that Jesus Christ has brought humankind back into union with Himself.

---

[4] *Oxford English Dictionary.*

> God was in Christ reconciling the world to Himself,
> we implore *you* on Christ's behalf, be reconciled to
> God. (2 Corinthians 5:19–20)

The only difference between us and those to whom we preach is that we already know what God has done for humankind through Christ, and they do not yet know.

1.2 THE GREAT COMMISSION

The ministry of Jesus Christ was recorded in the Synoptic Gospels, which were to be accomplished by all His disciples in their time and continued from generation to generation. Jesus Christ specifically gave the directive to go "preach," "teach," "baptize," and "disciple" people of all ages and nations. This is known as "the Great Commission."

> Go ye therefore and teach all nations, baptizing
> them in the name of the Father, and of the Son,
> and of the Holy Ghost: Teaching them to observe
> all things whatsoever I have commanded you: and,
> lo, I am with you always, even on to the end of the
> world. Amen. (Mat. 28:19–20 KJV)

> And He said to them, "Go into all the world and
> preach the Gospel to every creature. He who
> believes and is baptized will be saved; but he
> who does not believe will be condemned." (Mark
> 16:15–16)

Baptism is very important because it is a symbol of participation in Christ's death and resurrection. According to *Baptism, Eucharist, and Ministry,* written by the World Council of Churches, "Baptism means participating in the life, death and resurrection of Jesus Christ."[5] The commission to evangelize is also buttressed by the account of St. Luke:

> Repentance and remission of sins should be preached in His name to all nations, beginning at Jerusalem. And you are witnesses of these things. (Luke 24:47–48)

Obviously, these Gospelers have been able to obtain from the Lord what is known as "the Great Commission," and they have also been able to document and pass it from generation to generation. The undeniable focus is drawn at spreading the good news, preaching the Word of God, proclaiming the Gospel, witnessing to people, discipling them, and disseminating the good tidings.

This injunction to proclaim the Gospel stems from scripture:

> God so loved the world that He gave His only Son, that whoever believes in Him should not perish but have eternal life. For God sent the Son into the world, not to condemn the world but that the world might be saved through Him. (Jn. 3:16–17)

---

[5] *Baptism, Eucharist, and Ministry,* Faith and Order Paper No. 111 (World Council of Churches, Geneva, 1982), 2.

That is the good news, the good tidings, and the Gospel. That is the Great Commission.

God loves all—the whole world—including all sinners. He knew our condition of depravity, our weakness, and our helplessness.

> For when we were still without strength, in due time Christ died for the ungodly. For scarcely for a righteous man will one die; yet perhaps for a good man someone would even dare to die. But God demonstrates His own love toward us, in that while we were still sinners, Christ died for us. (Rom. 5:6–8)

God sent His only begotten Son into the world so that we might live through Him. In this is love, not that we loved God, but that He loved us and sent His Son to be the propitiation for our sins (1 John 4:9–10).

God makes adequate provision for the forgiveness of our sins. The law, at its own time, came in to increase the trespass, but where sin increased, grace abounded all the more. Therefore, through the abundance of God's love, all our sins were atoned for. God's provision in Christ's atonement makes us new. We should spread this wonderful grace that is free for everyone. James Schellman says, "The life of our communities of faith needs to attend to issues of maintenance but to be driven by issues of mission."[6] Mission

---

[6] James M. Schellman: "Initiation: Forming Disciples for Christ's Mission in the World," *Liturgy and Justice: To Worship God in Spirit and Truth,* ed. Anne Y. Koester (2002), 130.

should be our main focus. We take care of maintenance to be able to spread the Gospel.

Jesus Christ gives power to those who carry out the Great Commission. Power is not for self-aggrandizement. He gives power for effectiveness in ministry:

> Unless you people see signs and wonders, you will by no means believe. (Jn. 4:48)

The power is for service:

> You shall receive power when the Holy Spirit has come upon you; and you shall be witnesses to Me in Jerusalem, and in all Judea and Samaria, and to the end of the earth. (Acts 1:8)

Great manifestations of signs and wonders were testified by Barnabas and Paul:

> Then all the multitude kept silent and listened to Barnabas and Paul declaring how many miracles and wonders God had worked through them among the Gentiles. (Acts 15:12)

As people see miracles, signs, and wonders, it becomes easy for them to believe, repent, and offer themselves for baptism. Christ then forgives their sins, and as the Great Physician, He heals their diseases and sets them free. Those who believe are set free on earth and in His kingdom. He is preparing another kingdom for them, and He will take them there at the consummation of time.

Salvation is for all—as many as hear the Word and act—for whoever shall call on the Lord shall be saved:

> For the promise is to you and to your children, and to all who are afar off, as many as the Lord our God will call. (Acts 2:39)

> Then those who gladly received his word were baptized; and that day about three thousand souls were added to them. (Acts 2:41)

Jesus Christ can never lose His power. Christ is the same yesterday, today, and forever, and He has given us the power to spread the good news:

> Go into all the world and preach the Gospel to every creature. He who believes and is baptized will be saved; but he who does not believe will be condemned. And these signs will follow those who believe: In My name they will cast out demons; they will speak with new tongues; they will take up serpents; and if they drink anything deadly, it will by no means hurt them; they will lay hands on the sick, and they will recover. (Mark 16:15–18)

The Great Commission is rendered in the Gospel of Matthew 28:18–20:

> And Jesus came and spoke to them, saying, "All authority has been given to Me in heaven and on

earth. Go therefore and make disciples of all the nations, baptizing them in the name of the Father and of the Son and of the Holy Spirit, teaching them to observe all things that I have commanded you; and lo, I am with you always, even to the end of the age." (Mat. 28:18–20)

The early disciples took it very seriously, and as they went about preaching the Gospel of the kingdom, Jesus was with them with signs, wonders, miracles, healing, and the emancipation of people from the kingdom of darkness.

And they went out and preached everywhere, the Lord working with them and confirming the word through the accompanying signs. Amen. (Mk. 16:20)

1.3 A Brief Review of Church History on Evangelism

Evangelism has been the main focus of the church right from the beginning. The early church understood the commission that Christ gave to her. Jesus's Word was clear to them: "As the Father has sent me, even so I send you" (Jn. 20:21). As Roger Bowen said,

Evangelism describes the activity of making people disciples of Jesus Christ by the proclamation of the Gospel, so the Christians of the early age understood that they were to preach the Gospel to every creature, every race, every color, every tongue. They were sent, and they went. They were very zealous about it, considering the shortness of time. They were mindful of the fact that Jesus would soon return. With all seriousness, they moved out, over the hills, over the mountains, down the valleys, and into the villages, towns, and caves. They evangelized across the Mediterranean, North Africa, and South Europe, braving storms and contrary weather, perils on the sea, dangers on the land, overcoming all hazards. They were forging ahead without electricity, television, radio, public address systems, vehicles to carry them and the revival equipment, cars, or bicycles. However, they moved on happily, discharging their duty to the Master, Jesus Christ, who sent them.[7]

The second century witnessed a derailment of Christianity into theological controversy, which led to doctrinal tussles rather than moving forward. They weren't charting camel caravans into the Sahara or into African jungles or pressing eastward beyond the continental mountain barriers or northward to pagan tribes. They were more interested in conserving what they had than pressing on to the "uttermost part."

By the third century, the church had sunk into real apostasy. The fourth century saw her completely swept into a thousand years of spiritual darkness.

---

[7] Roger Bowen, "So I Send You: A Study Guide to Mission," SPCK. *International Study Guide*, 34.

In later years, Martin Luther came onto the scene and discovered "the just shall live by faith."[8] That was where Evangelical Reformation took place. The church began to trace her steps back to the early church evangelism. John and Charles Wesley with holiness and sanctification brought sanctity back into the church. The twentieth-century revival of the baptism of the Holy Ghost was a further step in the gradual renewal of the church.

From God's viewpoint, these truths were unveiled afresh so that true Christians might be empowered to witness "in all the world," among "all nations," to "every creature," thus putting to shame the power of darkness and opening the heavens for many souls to enter.

1.4 THE LOGIC OF EVANGELISM

Whatever evangelism might be, it is at least intimately related to the Gospel of the reign of God that was inaugurated in the life, death, and resurrection of Jesus Christ of Nazareth. Any vision of evangelism that ignores the kingdom of God, relegates it to a position of secondary importance, or fails to wrestle thoroughly with its content is destined from the outset to fail.[9] The kingdom of God is absolutely central to the ministry of Jesus Christ and to the mission of the disciples who launched the Christian movement into historical popularity. At stake is the fundamental theological

---

[8] Alister E. McGrath, *Christian Theology: An Introduction,* third Ed. "Luther on Justification," 2001, 455.

[9] W. J. Abraham, *The Logic of Evangelism.* (Great Britain: Hodder and Stoughton, 1999).

horizon within which both Jesus and His followers conceived and carried out the first paradigmatic evangelistic action of the church. This cannot be the last word; it must be the first word on evangelism.

First, it is noteworthy to know that the kingdom is already here. The expressions of Jesus and the early church about the kingdom of God and the reign of God showed different directions, for the future and for the present. The prophets spoke of God as the King of Israel and all the earth.

When John the Baptist appeared on the scene in Galilee, he spoke in a context that was laden with eschatological expectancy. He announced the arrival of the coming One and called the people of Israel to baptism and repentance. Jesus endorsed John's ministry and began a ministry of his own, ultimately leading to His death at the hands of the authorities. In the traditions that enshrine the earliest witness to His activity, we find ample evidence for the claim that Jesus—and the disciples who gathered around Him—were convinced that the reign of God had already dawned.

The evangelists witnessed through Jesus that the dynamic reign of God had appeared in His life. In narrating His story, the evangelists indicated that both His teachings and deeds were saturated by the reign of God appearing in history. Jesus's teachings, as enshrined in the scriptures, bear witness to the dawning of the kingdom of God in the present. Mark's summary of the teachings of Jesus Christ (Mk. 1:15) insists that the kingdom of God has arrived. The exorcisms Jesus practiced also suggest that the kingdom is now present (Mt. 12:28; Lk. 11:20). John the Baptist saw the miracles and healings as witnesses that He who was to come is here now

(Mt. 11:5–6; Lk. 7:22–23). A variety of comparisons suggest that the kingdom is already here and that the blessing of salvation is now available.

Conversely, the kingdom of God is yet to come. It is true that the kingdom has already come, but it is also true that it is yet to come in the future. Thus, the disciples are taught to petition God: "Thy kingdom come" (Mat. 6:9–13, Lk. 11:2–4). The beatitudes are shot through with the future hope of full satisfaction in the kingdom of God (Mt. 5:3–12; 6:20–23). Moreover, Jesus looks forward to a future day when many will come from East and West and sit at a table with Abraham in the kingdom of heaven (Mt. 8:11). Various statements about entry into the kingdom clearly imply a future coming of the kingdom that is yet to be realized: "Not everyone who says to Me, 'Lord, Lord' will enter the kingdom of heaven" (Mt. 7:21). The rich will find it difficult to enter (Mk. 10:25). These phrases indicate that, though the kingdom of God has arrived, the future aspect of it is yet to be revealed.

One of the most important passages that speaks of the kingdom of God as a future event is commonly referred to as the Olivet discourse. All three Synoptic Gospels refer to an apocalyptic consummation when the Son of Man will come in glory to gather His elect (Mk. 13:1–36; Mt. 24:1–51; Lk. 21:5–36). This event is described as that which will shake the natural order, resulting in the judgment and establishment of the perfect kingdom of God. It is to be preceded by the appearance of an evil personage and a terrible time of tribulations, which Luke explicitly depicts as a siege of Jerusalem and a historical judgment upon the Jewish nation.

How does the kingdom of God affect evangelism? It contributes to the spread of the Gospel. These events were also enough to provide the early community with its primary motivation for evangelism. Christianity began as a kind of renewal within Judaism. This is in keeping with the eschatological setting outlined above: the Gospel was for the Jews first. From the outset, they were destined to have a universal role in the redemption of the world. Thus, the kingdom that Jesus inaugurated began in Israel and was established by the restoration of Israel (symbolized in the calling of the twelve disciples).

In the early church, the Gospel spread—and the church grew because of the sovereign hand of God being in the midst of a community surrounded by people who were puzzled and intrigued by what they were seeing. This overwhelming impression created the traditions witnessing to the early evangelistic activity of the disciples and that the Holy Spirit was present in the community, beginning in the reign of God and inspiring the disciples to speak boldly of the mighty acts of salvation that God had wrought through the life, death, and resurrection of Jesus Christ.

1.5 What Prompted Me to Write This Book

Church fragmentation and denominational proliferation have been on an exponential and alarming increase all over the nations without any appreciable breakthrough in evangelism. The current schism that is bedeviling the United Methodist Church, especially in the United States of America, is a thing of great concern. When schism wanted to destroy the Methodist Church in Nigeria, God raised the Methodist Evangelical Movement (MEM), which brought about the reunification. Through MEM, evangelism spread all over Nigeria, many churches were planted, and the spiritual life of the church was revived. The golden jubilee of MEM in June 2023 is a joyful moment of thankfulness to God and for the work to advance more. We cannot afford to see the disintegration of the church of Christ.

Imagine your father having a big project, but you do not like how some of your siblings are doing it. Is running away from your father's project the answer? The separation and denominational fragmentation of churches have affected the unity of the church and the effectiveness of evangelism. The Gospel is being misrepresented, making it difficult for unbelievers to see any difference between churches as they fight and split from one another. The so-called converts from the establishing of new denominations are not usually the sinners repenting from their sins and coming into the family of God or the backslidden ones restored in their faith. Instead, they are Christians from various existing denominations who are influenced here and there to establish other congregations.

I am not trying to oppose the establishment of new Christian organizations if they are God-directed and Holy Spirit-led ones, but that would lead to the extension of Christ's kingdom without any prejudice. I am so thankful to God for the inspiration given to Bishop Thomas J. Bickerton—the resident bishop of New York's Annual Conference of the United Methodist Church and the president of the Council of Bishops Worldwide—for establishing cooperative parishes in the New York Annual Conference. I see this as a step forward in developing our mission, vision, and core values.

This will also strengthen our connectional engagements to reach out in unity to our communities with the Gospel of Jesus Christ for the transformation of the world.

We are living at a time when theology is being reduced to mere ideology. People are opting for ideological faith, and universal issues are taking over their minds. Confident preaching has already been replaced with polite reports in many circles. The church has lost her first love and needs to be reminded, reawakened and re-empowered. The church needs to be reenvisioned. "Where there is no vision, the people perish." Where there is no evangelism, the church crumbles.

These are the days when people are fond of traveling more than travailing, and they have no spiritual birth. Cecil Williamson noted that Islam is spreading like fire around the world.[10] The Muslims have also established mosques in Britain and in America, a thing that would never have been possible in the past. Hinduism, Baha'ism, Mormonism, Confucianism, Unitarianism, Christadelphianism, Rosicrucianism, Theosophy, Russelism, Spiritualism, Christian Science, Unitarianism, Seventh Day Adventism, and Modernism are expanding and drawing away the hearts of people from the kingdom of God. This is not a matter of bigotry; we need to fulfill the commission the Lord handed over to us.

According to Cecil Williamson, out of six billion people in the world, only two billion have confessed that Jesus is the Son of God. Another two billion people have yet to hear for the first time about Jesus Christ, and four billion have yet to decide for Christ.

---

[10] C. Williamson, "Good News Article: You Can Make a Difference," delivered at the Ministers' Conference, Sagamu, 1999 (unpublished).

The church must shift her attention to this primary assignment of evangelizing the world without further delay. For this sin-hungry age, we need an evangelism-hungry church. Therefore, a topic like this is needed to arouse the minds of all believers to this neglected task: Evangelism.

2

THE ESSENTIALS OF
EVANGELISM

Spreading the Gospel is handled—not just by anybody—but by equipped bona fide members of the body of Christ. One must qualify to meet the demands of the Spirit-controlled service of leading others to Christ. As Christians, we are called to spread the good news of Jesus Christ to all corners of the earth. This is not just an option for us; it is our bounding duty and responsibility.

Jesus Christ, our Savior, tells us in the Gospel of Mark 16:15: "Go into all the world and preach the Gospel to every creature." This is a command. This is a mandate to go. We are sent out into the world to evangelize. So, what are the essentials of evangelism? First, we need to have a clear understanding of the Gospel. The Gospel is the good news of salvation through faith in Jesus Christ. We need to understand that we are all sinners and that we cannot save ourselves. It is only through faith in Jesus Christ that we can be saved. We must be able to articulate this message clearly and succinctly so that others can understand it.

Second, there is a need to have a heart for evangelism. We must be passionate about sharing the Gospel with others. This means that we are intentional in our outreach efforts. We are willing to step out of our comfort zones and engage with people who may not look like us or believe like us.

Third, we need to be equipped for evangelism. This means that we must be knowledgeable about the Bible and its teachings. We must be able to answer common questions that people may have about Christianity. We must be able to share our own personal testimonies of how Christ has transformed our lives.

Fourth, we must be prayerful in our evangelism efforts. We need to pray for opportunities to share the Gospel with the people and show love to those we are trying to reach so that their hearts are open to receiving the message of Christ. We must be willing to persevere in our evangelism efforts. We may face rejection and ridicule, but we need to remember that we are doing the work of the Lord. We need to be persistent in our outreach efforts, trusting that God will use our efforts for His glory.

Evangelism is an essential part of our Christian faith. We need to have a clear understanding of the Gospel, a heart for evangelism, be equipped for evangelism, be prayerful in our evangelism efforts, and be willing to persevere in our outreach efforts. The four Cs of the essentials of evangelism are conversion, conviction, commission, and compassion.[11]

---

[11] W. F. Kumuyi, *Complete Bible Study Series in One Volume*, 46.

2.1 AN EVANGELIST MUST HAVE THE ASSURANCE OF CONVERSION

An evangelist must first experience—and then show forth—thorough *conversion*. An unconverted "soul winner" (a so-called Christian who does not get a definite testimony of conversion) is like a blind person trying to explain the beauty of colors! How can you proclaim a Savior you have never met? Preaching about who you do not know leads to heresy and wrong doctrines that abound all around us. True evangelists must be sure of their conversion before taking up any Gospel work.

How can one get converted? Peter sheds light on it as he says, "Repent therefore and be converted, that your sins may be blotted out, so that times of refreshing may come from the presence of the Lord" (Acts 3:19). This shows that the issue of sin has to be settled for conversion to take effect. One must repent from all sins and turn completely to God before the time of refreshing can come from the presence of the Lord. This repentance must wholly depend on the atoning blood of Jesus Christ, which is able to wash the vilest sinner clean.

In order to be saved, one must confess the Lord Jesus orally and believe in the heart that God has raised Him from the dead (Rom. 10:9–10). Through the ages, those who have sincerely taken these steps have had proven testimonies and have been able to make an impact in Gospel work. For instance, the conversion of Paul the apostle produced a distinct and drastic change in his life. A great persecutor of the Way became a great preacher of the Gospel (Acts 9:26–29).

2.2 An Unshakable Conviction

True evangelists must have a strong, unshakable *conviction*. Certainty is brought to their minds for every biblical truth unveiled to them. Persons with clear conviction devote all their time, talents, strength, and money to the furtherance of the Gospel. There must be a strong conviction about God and the Bible about Christ, His humanity and divinity, His coming to the world and suffering, His death and resurrection, His ascension and Second Coming, the new heaven and the new earth, and other truths revealed in the Holy Writ. This certainty in the inner mind of true evangelists makes them readily obey the command to evangelize the world.

Our understanding of the nature of God and Christian faith will have an enormous influence on the way we are sharing the faith, reaching out to others, and the quality of the Gospel we carry about. The Gospel passes through culture and imbibes things from it.[12] There are different denominations, and there are different types of spirituality: Episcopal spirituality, Anglican spirituality, Methodist spirituality, Christ Apostolic Church spirituality, Baptist spirituality, et cetera. However, evangelism has no alternate versions. The truth once overemphasized becomes heresy. Therefore, one must diligently search the scriptures to ensure one's conviction is purely based on biblical facts before blowing out the trumpet.

Some people's feelings have been injured; others have been exploited by a brand of oppressive evangelism that has succeeded in creating nothing but guilt and resentment within them. Knowing

---

[12] J. A. Bamgboye, Evangelism Hand-Out. ICT, Ibadan (1997) (unpublished).

fully well that the purpose of evangelism is persuasion and not denunciation, one must balance the truth and the application of love in the approach.

2.3 A Real Evangelist Has Consciously Received the Great Commission

The real evangelist has imperatively received the Great Commission. Such a person is not just the one who has had or known about the need and the call. He is the one who has accepted the great responsibility. He is a preacher because he has received Christ's Commission and not because the Public Service Commission cannot find him a job!

For such an evangelist, the Great Commission is not received based on personal momentary gains or sensual emolument. There are people who have these behind their minds in setting up the Gospel work. They look for ways of exploiting people in order to accumulate wealth. They draw money and materials from people for their personal enjoyment. They siphon wealth from the poor—pepper sellers, salt sellers, et cetera—to build mansions for themselves. Some other brands of evangelists are out for the purpose of the prestige and honor accruable from the Gospel work. They rate themselves above all others. Pride and pomposity are their identity.

All these are not the interest of an evangelist who has truly received the Great Commission. All his concern is this: "Seek first His kingdom and His righteousness." It is on the course of faithfully discharging your duty that "all these things," the blessings, "shall be yours as well" (Mat. 6:33). When we take care of our character and the Gospel that is entrusted into our hands in all humility and obedience, prestige and honor will follow. Therefore, such an evangelist "will most gladly spend and be spent" for the salvation of souls into the kingdom of God—and the person will be duly rewarded because God does not owe any one anything (2 Cor. 12:15; Lk. 6:38). Many so-called Evangelists and pastors have different motives than that of the real Commission given by Jesus Christ, our Savior. They do all the other things, but they neglect the Great Commission. Their motive may be accumulation of wealth, making a name, becoming popular, or being influential in society.

A true evangelist has received the Great Commission to "go" and make disciples of all nations. This vocation is specific, definite, clear, and unambiguous. This does not include personal interest. The idea of evangelism did not originate from humans.[13] God is the Initiator. It is God's idea. God-self is the first Evangelist. God's nature shows that God is a seeking God. That is why Jesus came down from glory and took the form of a man to dwell with us: Emmanuel!

God is a missionary God, a sending God. God started by sending God's own beloved Son from heaven to come and deliver us from the power of sin and death. This work Christ did and accomplished on the cross where He was nailed. He died and resurrected victoriously. Before His ascension into heaven, He left the legacy of faith-sharing for all people who believe in Him to "go

---

[13] E. Fox and G. Morris, *Faith-Sharing. Dynamic Christian Witnessing by Invitation*, 1996.

into all the world and preach the Gospel to every creature" (Mk. 16:15).

> Go therefore and make disciples of all the nations, baptizing them in the name of the Father and of the Son and of the Holy Spirit, teaching them to observe all things that I have commanded you. (Mat. 28:19–20ᵃ)

> And you shall be witnesses to Me in Jerusalem, and in all Judea and Samaria, and to the end of the earth. (Acts 1:8ᵇ)

The Commission is straightforward.

The injunction to "go" is binding for all believers, and the saying of Paul is applicable to all of us: "For necessity is laid upon me; yes, woe is me if I do not preach the Gospel!" (1 Cor. 9:16). It is not a matter of saying, "If I like, I may evangelize." The human souls are tied on your neck, and they must not go to hell because of your negligence.

> God said, "When I say to the wicked, 'O wicked man, you shall surely die!' and you do not speak to warn the wicked from his way, that wicked man shall die in his iniquity; but his blood I will require at your hand. Nevertheless if you warn the wicked to turn from his way, and he does not turn from his way, he shall die in his iniquity; but you have delivered your soul." (Ezekiel 33:8–9)

This much emphasis shows the strong string attached to the importance of spreading the good news so that people will not perish:

> Break up your fallow ground, for it is time to seek
> the Lord, till He comes and rains righteousness on
> you. (Hos. 10–12[b])

God has always taken the initiative of bringing sinners back to Himself in repentance and forsaking of their old way. To evangelize is to spur to spiritual consciousness and to arouse recovery of life, vigor, and strength. It is to stimulate rising from a state of ignorance, negligence, disuse, languor, depression, or discouragement. The Holy Spirit makes a real evangelist perceive the depraved conditions of sinners, and this gives them the impetus and the zeal to launch out in quest of the lost souls.

2.4 CHRISTLIKE COMPASSION

A deep, burning Christlike compassion compels a true evangelist to sacrifice all that is necessary for the salvation of others. Compassion is an essential ingredient of evangelism. Have it and succeed; neglect it and fall!

The measure of one's compassion is the sacrifices one makes, the effectual fervent prayers one offers, the long, tireless journeys one makes, the much patience one takes with others to persuade, convince, and help them, the tears one genuinely sheds, the earnest speeches and invitation to Christ one gives, and the hardship one endures for the souls of others.

Jesus Christ, our perfect example, was full of compassion. He went about doing good, setting the captives free, binding up the brokenhearted, healing the sick, comforting all who mourned, and opening the prisons to those who were bound.

> But when He saw the multitudes, He was moved with compassion for them, because they were weary and scattered, like sheep having no shepherd. (Mat. 9:36)

Jesus was always prompted to help. He was always feeling for the sufferings of others. When He departed to a desert place, many people who had problems sought after him to receive help.

> And when Jesus went out, He saw a great multitude; and He was moved with compassion for them, and healed their sick. (Mat. 14:14)

Two blind men who craved help were also blessed.

> So, Jesus had *compassion* on them, and touched their eyes and immediately their eyes received sight, and they followed Him. (Mat. 20:34)

A leper who came to him, beseeching him for cleansing, was not rejected either.

> Then Jesus, moved with compassion, stretched out His hand and touched him, and said to him, "I am willing. Be cleansed." (Mk. 1:41)

We need Christlike *compassion* to succeed in the work of evangelism. A landmark of success made by Paul in the Gospel work could not have been possible if he was not soaked in a burning, deep compassion.

The same Paul has this confession to make:

> I tell the truth in Christ, I am not lying, my conscience also bearing me witness in the Holy Spirit, that I have great sorrow and continual grief in my heart. For I could wish that I myself were accursed from Christ for my brethren, my countrymen according to the flesh. (Rom. 9:1–3)

It is obvious that Paul was overwhelmed with travailing compassion for the salvation of his kinsmen, the Israelites. He earnestly declared the desire of his heart concerning them:

> Brethren, my heart's desire and prayer to God for Israel is that they may be saved. (Rom. 10:1)

Because of his deep, heartfelt compassion, he was able to go on an aggressive evangelism, coming against all who could hinder his success.

Without this great compassion, we cannot make a difference. Jesus had it—and He still has it—and He made a wonderful breakthrough in His ministry. Paul was intoxicated with it, and he shook the earth. Peter, James, and John launched out compassionately and were able to spread the good news all around in their time:

And on some have compassion, making a
distinction; but others save with fear, pulling them
out of the fire, hating even the garment defiled by
the flesh. (Jude 22–23)

Gospel communication is neglected today because we are
barren of divine compassion. The fearful bondage and slavery that
exist in the world today and threaten the rest of humankind are no
fairy tales! People in these trying days need mercy. The sick, the
sad, and the less privileged need help. In these days of darkness,
incandescent children of God are needed to bring the light of
victory over darkness.

Alas! There is no more compassion and no more mercy. There
is not as much evangelism as we used to have it. Most of what people
do today is commercialized Gospel, which does not pay for this
degenerate generation. At the moment, a rushing mighty wind of
false religions and lukewarm Christianity is lashing the world.[14]
On the other hand, warned of false fire by fireless people, we often
settle for no fire at all! Where is soul-awakening, heartwarming,
compassionate preaching? May God help the nations ruined with
man-made religions in this night of blight and plight.

---

[14] L. Ravenhill, *Why Revival Tarries* (England: Send the Light Trust, 1972).

3

THE SCRIPTURAL PATTERN
OF EVANGELISM

3.1 TYPES OF EVANGELISM

Basically, there are two types of evangelism in the New Testament: *personal evangelism* and *mass evangelism.*

All believers are called to be fishers of souls, fishing either with a great net (mass evangelism) or with a single hook at a time (personal evangelism).[15] Laymen and laywomen are relinquishing the work of evangelism to the clergy in the church, neglecting the Great Commission.

In a war faced by an army, what would happen if all the fighting were left to the commanding officers? What would be the end result of a fishing company if all the fishing on the sea and marketing were left to the general manager alone? Obviously, no success could be recorded with such an arrangement. What would happen if the acres of crops ripened and the work of harvesting was left to the

---

[15] W. F. Kumuyi, "Complete Bible Study Series in one volume," 47–52 (unpublished).

head of the household alone—and the others were folding their hands? Of course, there would be a lot of waste.

3.1.1 Mass Evangelism

Mass evangelism focuses attention on many people at a time.[16] This could be done from the perspective of the ministries of evangelism:

- crusade evangelism
- local church evangelism
- rural evangelism
- urban evangelism
- industrial evangelism
- child evangelism
- student evangelism
- family or group visitation evangelism
- women evangelism
- film evangelism
- music evangelism

The common factor in these ministries' evangelism is that many people are reached at a time with the good news—just as many fish are caught at a time when fishing nets are used. It then remains that sorting must be done immediately after hauling in the nets. If a single person is approached, for example, a single child or a student, then it is personal evangelism. Depending on the approach, some of the above items may be categorized as mass

---

[16] J. A. Bamgboye. "Evangelism Paper" I.C.T., Ibadan, Nigeria (unpublished).

or personal evangelism. When two or more people are reached at a time, that is mass evangelism. The extent of mass evangelism can go from few people to millions of people. A small auditorium can be used in some cases, but other situations might require a large stadium filled with as many people as possible.

3.1.2 Personal Evangelism

As we read through the Gospels, it is amazing to note how Jesus devoted so much more time to individuals than to crowds. He met with the woman of Samaria at the well and conversed with her until she was convinced and believed. He ministered to Nicodemus, a ruler of the Jews, and supplied answers to the questions, agitating his mind. A man born blind had an encounter with Him, and his eyes were opened.

Many individuals at one time or another were met as such and were duly satisfied. For instance, the encounter of the woman of Samaria with Jesus at the well in John 4 is a perfect example of personal evangelism. It is a powerful reminder of how Jesus reached out to those who were marginalized and considered outcasts by society. Heather Murray Elkins said, "Some are saturated with toxic levels of violence and inhumanity."[17] In this encounter with the Samaritan woman, we see Jesus breaking cultural barriers and demonstrating how we should evangelize to those who are lost and searching for meaning in their lives.

The story begins with Jesus and His disciples passing through Samaria. Jesus, tired and thirsty, stops at a well to rest while His

---

[17] Heather Murray Elkins, *Worshiping Women: Re-Forming God's People for Praise* (Nashville: Abingdon Press, 1994), 42.

disciples go to buy food. He meets a Samaritan woman who comes to draw water from the well. This encounter is significant because Jews and Samaritans did not associate with each other due to long-standing religious and cultural differences.

Despite these differences, Jesus engages in a conversation with the woman and offers her living water. Finding living water has been the desire of every thirsty, suffering, and disenfranchised person. Heather Murray Elkins[4] observed that the Samaritan woman asks Jesus the same question, and Jesus explains that it is not physical water but the Holy Spirit, which provides eternal life.[18] As their conversation continues, Jesus reveals that he knows about the woman's troubled past. Despite this, He offers her forgiveness and salvation.

The way Jesus evangelizes to this woman is a powerful example of how we should reach out to those who are lost and searching for meaning in their lives. Here are a few key takeaways from this encounter:

- First, we must be willing to break cultural barriers. Just as Jesus engaged with the Samaritan woman despite the cultural differences, we too must be willing to engage with those who may be different from us in terms of their race, ethnicity, or culture. We should not allow these differences to prevent us from sharing the love of Christ.
- Second, we must be willing to offer genuine care and compassion. Jesus took the time to engage in a conversation with this woman and offer her living water. We also must

---

[18] Ibid.

be willing to listen to the needs of others and offer genuine care and compassion.

- Third, we must be willing to address the root issues of people's lives. Jesus knew about the woman's troubled past, and He offered her forgiveness and salvation. We also must be willing to address the root issues in people's lives and offer them the hope and healing that comes through a relationship with Christ.

- Fourth, we must be willing to offer people the truth. Jesus did not shy away from the truth, but He spoke it in love. We also must be willing to share the truth of the Gospel with others—even if it is uncomfortable or unpopular.

Personal evangelism is the person-to-person sharing of the good news of salvation with the aim of leading the sinner to repentance and wholly surrendering to God through Jesus Christ. The purpose of personal evangelism is to bring individuals into a personal, experiential knowledge of Jesus Christ as their Savior and Lord and not to accept a particular creed, join a church, form a group, or become a moralist.

Personal evangelism, like mass evangelism, is a costly ministry in the sense that it requires sacrifice, self-denial, and discipline. Samuel Cetuk said, "Society today is more complex, fast changing, and secularized compared to that of fifty years ago."[19] When the early church sent out the first preachers (Acts 13), the Holy Spirit did not select people needed least by the

---

[19] Virginia Samuel Cetuk, *What to Expect in Seminary: Theological Education as Spiritual Formation* (Nashville: Abingdon Press, 1998), 140–41.

church. Real conversion, sound convictions, divine commission, deep burning compassion, and strong courage are indispensable necessities for anyone who wants to be truly used by God in reaching the lost with the Gospel.

The need to reach all categories of people—young and old, American, Indian, Nigerian, white and black, and male and female—must be recognized. The Gospel must be spread to the young ones, especially, before Satan confirms them in unbelief, darkness, and evil. They must be captured with the love of God and be nurtured with the Gospel before the years carry them away from the truth.

The young mind is an agile, changing, expanding thing that is always open to outside influences. To be effective in teaching the young and obtain results, one must keep in mind:

1. The law of readiness: It is easiest for each one to learn something when they are interested and ready to learn. The evangelists should create an interest for spiritual things.
2. The law of exercise: Learning is best enhanced through effective participation and doing. It is better to give an opportunity to pray than to give a young mind a long talk on prayer.
3. The law of satisfaction: To keep anyone's interest going, the person must have satisfaction. They must have their needs satisfied.

Every message must contain God's sacrificial love for humans' guilt for sins committed, Christ's atonement on the cross, and humans' need for repentance and faith in Christ.

3.1.3 The Urgent Need to Reach Young People with the Gospel

There is an urgent need to capture the young souls with the love of God and nurture them with the Gospel before their hearts are carried away by the sleights of the devil. The hearts of the young ones are very soft and malleable and can easily be turned around. That is why we must show them the way of the Lord before the years roll them into worldliness. The evangelist must go into the busy world of young people and preach the Gospel because each one is a precious and unique part of God's creation. Evangelism among the youth is of extreme importance.

> That our sons may be as plants grown up in their youth; That our daughters may be as pillars, sculptured in palace style; Happy are the people who are in such a state; Happy are the people whose God is the Lord! (Psalm 144:12, 15)

The young mind is an agile, expanding entity that is always open to outside influences. That is why it grows very fast in the early stages of life. To be effective in teaching the young and obtaining results, we must keep these facts in mind.

First, we must understand that learning is enhanced when there is interest. It is easiest for each one to learn something when one is interested and ready to learn. Because I studied music—and it has become my special area—I play for my church free of charge as a pastor. The church does not need to hire an organist, and because members love the way I play, some of them approached me and begged me to train their children in music. I promised I would do that if some of them were interested. Eventually, I scheduled weekly lessons for seven of them. I asked them to buy some books, which they all did.

When the lessons started, they all came joyfully. As I started the rudiments with them, the exercise seemed boring for them. After the third week, some of them stopped coming. I understood the reason, but I was determined to play some pieces of music for them during class. Yes, it worked! Their interest increased, and they began enjoying the sessions. Those who stopped coming returned, and the lessons became interesting. If we want the young people to embrace the Gospel, we must create things that arouse their interest in spiritual things.

> Gather the people together, men and women and little ones, and the stranger who is within your gates, that they may hear and that they may learn to fear the Lord your God and carefully observe all the words of this law, and that their children, who have not known it, may hear and learn to fear the Lord your God as long as you live in the land which you cross the Jordan to possess. (Deut. 31:12–13)

We need to reach out to the young people for Christ before Satan confirms them in unbelief and the evils of the world. We must persuade them with the love of God and nurture them to maturity with the Gospel of Christ before Satan and sin carry them away.

Secondly, we must involve them in spiritual practices. We learn best through participating and doing. It is better to give them opportunities to pray, sing, share testimony, and read scripture than to sit idly.

> And these words which I command you today shall be in your heart. You shall teach them diligently to your children, and shall talk of them when you sit in your house, when you walk by the way, when you lie down, and when you rise up. You shall bind them as a sign on your hand, and they shall be as frontlets between your eyes. You shall write them on the doorposts of your house and on your gates. (Deut. 6:6–9)

God's instruction for all people, including the young people, is to keep God's Word in our hearts. This calls for people to hear the Word that God wants us to keep in our hearts. Hearing the Word develops our faith.

Thirdly, to be satisfied in the Word of God, people must have their needs met. The efficacy of God's Word brings miracles, which leads to satisfaction:

> And the Lord said, "Shall I hide from Abraham what I am doing, since Abraham shall surely become a great and mighty nation, and all the nations of the earth shall be blessed in him? For I have known him, in order that he may command his children and his household after him, that they keep the way of the Lord, to do righteousness and

justice, that the Lord may bring to Abraham what He has spoken to him." (Genesis 18:17–19)

For the promise is to you and to your children, and to all who are afar off, as many as the Lord our God will call. (Acts 2:39)

As we minister to young people, every message must contain God's sacrificial love for humanity, feelings of guilt for sins committed, Christ's atonement on the cross, the human need for repentance, and faith in Christ for forgiveness and redemption. We need to earnestly present the Gospel to the young ones to avoid losing them into the hands of the devil. The devil does not relent in his efforts. We cannot afford to yield this great multitude of children and youth to the devil! The scriptures reveal the effect of spreading the good news among them:

For "whoever calls on the name of the Lord shall be saved." How then shall they call on Him in whom they have not believed? And how shall they believe in Him of whom they have not heard? And how shall they hear without a preacher? And how shall they preach unless they are sent? As it is written: "How beautiful are the feet of those who preach the Gospel of peace, who bring glad tidings of good things!" So then faith comes by hearing, and hearing by the Word of God. (Rom. 10:13–15, 17)

In an attempt to get the Gospel to the young people, one should begin with an effort to understand the individuals. There is a tendency to decide that a certain person is good or bad by looking at their facial appearance or stature, but it is God who knows the heart. When we open up a conversation with an individual, God will reveal to us the direction to follow:

> He who heeds the word wisely will find good, and whoever trusts in the Lord, happy is he. The wise in heart will be called prudent, and sweetness of the lips increases learning. Understanding is a wellspring of life to him who has it. But the correction of fools is folly. The heart of the wise teaches his mouth, and adds learning to his lips. Pleasant words are like a honeycomb, Sweetness to the soul and health to the bones. There is a way that seems right to a man. But its end is the way of death. (Prov. 16:20–25)

Ecclesiastes 10:10 also tells us that "wisdom brings success." We must understand the prospect's religious, cultural, social, and mental background. Are there some pressures that are molding this person's attitudes and responses? Many people have feelings of distress, despondency, anxiety, a sense of incompleteness, and struggles about sexual interests. The concerned evangelist should know the sinner's needs, concerns, ideas, doubts, fears, et cetera in order to show them the way through to repentance and faith in Christ Jesus. They need to be loved, accepted, secure, spiritual, and successful.

For evangelists to realize their vision for winning young souls for Christ, they must observe the prospect's attitude toward spiritual things, establish a relationship based on friendship and trust, and share their own Christian experiences. They also need to present the plan of salvation to the prospect without forcing the issue. Let the individual know that all have sinned and fallen short of the glory of God (Rom. 3:23). Let the person understand that we cannot save ourselves (Eph 2:8–9; Acts 4:12). Declare with love to the prospect that the wages of sin is death (Rom. 6:23), but God loves the whole world and does not want anyone to perish (Jn. 3:16; Rom. 5:8). Therefore, all people need to confess their sins, ask for forgiveness, forsake them, repent, and accept Jesus as their personal Lord and Savior (1 John 1:8–9; Prov. 28:13; Acts 2:38; Rom. 10:9–11; Jn. 1:12). Then, you can answer questions frankly and sincerely and clear doubts patiently.

At this juncture, you will guide them to a personal experience with Christ. This involves arousing their interest, enlightening them, and encouraging them to respond to questions. Encourage them to testify before friends, classmates, coworkers, or parents. Help them grow in the Lord and mature spiritually as they grow physically. In order for new converts to grow in the grace and knowledge of our Lord and Savior, Jesus Christ, they must be praying and holding the promises of God by faith. They must cultivate the habit of praying every day and reading and studying the Bible with helpful notes. They must be engaging in personal evangelism, attending Christian fellowship regularly, and ensuring that they are integrated into a Bible-believing church.

3.2 The Urgency of Evangelism

3.2.1 The Harvest Truly Is Plentiful

We are living in a time characterized by "evil." Paul says in his epistle to the Galatians 1:4 that our Lord Jesus Christ gave Himself for our sins so that He might deliver us from this present evil world, according to the will of God and our Father. The days are evil.

> But know this, that in the last days perilous times will come: For men will be lovers of themselves, lovers of money, boasters, proud, blasphemers, disobedient to parents, unthankful, unholy, unloving, unforgiving, slanderers, without self-control, brutal, despisers of good, traitors, headstrong, haughty, lovers of pleasure rather than lovers of God. (2 Tim. 3:1–4)

This truly is a period of time marked by the dominion of Satan.

> Whose minds the god of this age has blinded, who do not believe, lest the light of the Gospel of the glory of Christ, who is the image of God, should shine on them. (2 Cor. 4:4a)

Jesus has come to save the lost, and these are ripe already.[20] Darkness has covered the land. We are in a period shadowed by darkness, ungodliness, and lust. The harvest truly is plentiful.

---

[20] L. Ravenhill, *Why Revival Tarries* (London: Send The Light Trust, 1972).

But when He (Jesus) saw the multitudes, He was moved with compassion for them, because they were weary and scattered, like sheep having no shepherd. Then He said to His disciples, "The harvest truly is plentiful, but the laborers are few." (Mat. 9:36–37).

When the harvest is ripe, delay causes waste:

Do you not say, "There are still four months and then comes the harvest"? Behold, I say to you, lift up your eyes and look at the fields, for they are already white for harvest! And he who reaps receives wages, and gathers fruit for eternal life, that both he who sows and he who reaps may rejoice together. (Jn. 4:35–36)

3.2.2 A Clarion Call to the Valley of Dry Bones

Ezekiel describes the place of a deserted mass evangelism:

The hand of the Lord came upon me and brought me out in the Spirit of the Lord, and set me down in the midst of the valley; and it was full of bones. Then He caused me to pass by them all around, and behold, there were very many in the open valley; and indeed they were very dry. And He said to me, "Son of man, can these bones live?" So I answered, "O Lord God, You know." Again He said to me, "Prophesy to these bones, and say to them, O dry bones, hear the word of the Lord! Thus says the Lord God to these bones: Surely I will cause breath to enter into you, and you shall live. I will put sinews on you and bring flesh upon you, cover you with skin and put breath in you; and you shall live. Then you shall know that I am the Lord." So I prophesied as I was commanded; and as I prophesied, there was a noise, and suddenly a rattling; and the bones came together, bone to bone. Indeed, as I looked, the sinews and the flesh came upon them, and the skin covered them over; but there was no breath in them. Also He said to me, "Prophesy to the breath, prophesy, son of man, and say to the breath, Thus says the Lord God: Come from the four winds, O breath, and breathe on these slain, that they may live." So I prophesied as He commanded me, and breath came into them, and they lived, and stood upon their feet, an exceedingly great army. (Ezek. 37:1–10)

The description of this audience is pathetic. God did not move Ezekiel from his position, but he was led in the Spirit to the valley of despondency. What situation can be as terrible as this? This is an embodiment of hopelessness! The dry bones depict that they had been there for a long time. They did not suddenly become dry bones. Nobody rescued them at the early stage of the problem. No preacher to warn them. No teacher to teach them. No helper, no one to proclaim the truth. No one. Wounds and putrefying sores developed into disease, and disease resulted in death. Death takes out life, and decay sets in. Skin, flesh, ligaments, and all the viscera decomposed, and bones emerged. The bones became disjointed and were scattered all over the valley.

As terrible as the situation was, God asked Ezekiel a question: "Can these bones live?" That was a great test! Ezekiel gave a careful answer to God. Looking at the situation superficially, one could have quickly said, "This is impossible!" But knowing that with God, nothing shall be impossible, the prophet answered, "O Lord God, You know." Power belongs to God, and when we follow God's instructions, nothing is impossible.

The Lord God said, "Prophesy." There were two words of prophecy Ezekiel was asked to pronounce: to prophesy to the dust and to prophesy to the Spirit. God did the work of creation in that valley of dry bones. That takes us back to the creation story:

> And the Lord God formed man of the dust of the
> ground, and breathed into his nostrils the breath of
> life; and man became a living being. (Genesis 2:7)

Here, the physical and the spiritual came into the equation.

I learned two important indices from this scenario: the word of prophecy and the pronouncement of the word of prophecy. The word of prophecy was given to Ezekiel:

> Surely I will cause breath to enter into you, and you
> shall live. I will put sinews on you and bring flesh
> upon you, cover you with skin and put breath in
> you; and you shall live. (Ezekiel 37:5–6)

For any miracle that will happen, we must live by the Word of God.

Scriptures are prophecies.

> For prophecy never had its origin in the human will, but prophets, though human, spoke from God as they were carried along by the Holy Spirit. (2 Pet. 1:21 NIV)

The scriptures encompass prophecies in all situations in life. Your problem may relate to sickness, disease, endemic, epidemic, pandemic, bondage, addiction, shelter, clothing, bad luck, or accident. There are prophecies that will unhook you from the problem in the Word of God, but there is another aspect of pronouncement of the prophecy. Because the Lord is the author and giver of the Word, one must be in a good relationship with Him.

The Lord told Ezekiel what to say: "O dry bones, hear the word of the Lord! Thus says the Lord God to these bones." That was exactly how God asked him to begin. Unfortunately, "Thus says the Lord" is not so much heard anymore among the children of God. "Hear the word of the Lord" is fast fading away from the lips of the exponents of the Gospel. That is why miracles, signs and wonders are not so evident among the people who are called servants of God.

When I was appointed to the church, I did not know the spiritual level of the members. However, the Lord led me to prophesy, and I said, "Thus says the Lord, there's somebody here who has a problem with his wife. The Lord asked me to pray with you—come out here."

Nobody came out!

I could sense people slighting my words. Then the Lord led me to say, "Thus says the Lord, the person is here this morning. The person was born in February 1975, and the wife is not in church. If you are the person, please come, the Lord is leading me to pray for you."

A man rushed to the front.

I said, "Were you born in 1975?"

He said, "Yes."

I said, "Were you born in February?"

He said, "Yes."

I said, "Did you have any quarrel with your wife at home?"

He said, "Yes!"

Even before all the questions landed, the entire church had been filled with spiritual energy. People were shouting praise to the Lord.

I prayed for him, and since that day, the man has been so thankful to the Lord and church members for having a positive mind about the words of prophecy.

God asked the prophet Ezekiel to prophesy:

> Hear the Word of the Lord! Thus says the Lord God to these bones: "Surely, I will cause breath to enter into you, and you shall live. I will put sinews on you and bring flesh upon you, cover you with skin and put breath in you; and you shall live. Then you shall know that I am the Lord. As I prophesied,

there was a noise, and suddenly a rattling; and the
bones came together, bone to bone." (Ezek. 37:5-7).

What did that produce? Skeletons! Can skeletons praise God?
No! Then continued prophet Ezekiel. As the prophecy advanced,
sinews came on the bones, flesh filled them, and they were covered
with skin. Hallelujah!! There appeared many corpses in the valley
that had been filled with scattered bones. But can corpses praise
the Lord? No! Without breath, no life. Job says, "The Spirit of
God has made me, and the breath of the Almighty gives me life"
(Job 33:4).

> Prophesy to the breath, prophesy, son of man,
> and say to the breath, "Thus says the Lord God:
> 'Come from the four winds, O breath, and breathe
> on these slain, that they may live.'" And Ezekiel
> said, "So I prophesied as He commanded me, and
> breath came into them, and they lived, and stood
> upon their feet, an exceedingly great army." (Ezek.
> 37:9-10)

There is an exceedingly great latter days' spiritual army that the
Lord is raising for the church. In the time of prophet Ezekiel, the
prophecy was concentrated on the people of Israel. If God could
do that for a nation, imagine what God is going to do for the entire
world. The harvest is ripe, and the laborers are few at the backdrop
of the preparation for the imminent coming of the Lord for the
rapture of the saints.

3.2.3 The Shortness of Time and the Endlessness of Eternity

Time is short. We cannot keep on neglecting the Great Commission:

> Jesus says, "I must work the works of Him who sent Me while it is day; the night is coming when no one can work." (Jn. 9:4)

This is the time we have to really propagate the Gospel and reach the unreached. We have moved far into this millennium, which we never thought of entering before the Rapture. It is a privilege to remain on this side of creation. We are nearer to the end than those in ages past. The imminent—soon, sudden, and unannounced—return of Christ is the hope and expectation of the church. This can happen at any time because we are living in the very last days of this dispensation.

The prophecies that are to be fulfilled only in the last days are being fulfilled before our very eyes.

> I charge you therefore before God and the Lord Jesus Christ, who will judge the living and the dead at His appearing and His kingdom: Preach the word! Be ready in season and out of season. Convince, rebuke, exhort, with all longsuffering and teaching. For the time will come when they will not endure sound doctrine, but according to their own desires, because they have itching ears, they will heap up for themselves teachers; and

they will turn their ears away from the truth, and
be turned aside to fables. But you be watchful in
all things, endure afflictions, do the work of an
evangelist, fulfill your ministry. (2 Tim. 4:1–5)

Every member of the church should be involved in aggressive
evangelism for the expansion of the kingdom of God, which is now
in preparation for eternity ahead.

The shortness of time should be of concern to every believer.
Paul discussed the issue of marriage with the Corinthian Christians:

But this I say, brethren, the time is short, so that
from now on even those who have wives should
be as though they had none, those who weep as
though they did not weep, those who rejoice as
though they did not rejoice, those who buy as
though they did not possess, and those who use
this world as not misusing it. For the form of this
world is passing away. (1 Cor. 7:29–31)

Paul was admonishing them to relish more of the things that
are of eternal value because this world is not permanent. The whole
world should be evangelized before Christ returns.

4

NEGLIGENCE OF THE GREAT COMMISSION

4.1 THE RELUCTANT EVANGELIST

When God wants to use a person, it takes time for the person to understand what God is about to do. The person may even have wandered away, lost in the rubble of life.

The life of Moses was full of turns and curves. Remember what surrounded his birth? He was born at a time of the persecution of the Hebrews in Egypt. Pharaoh decreed that every male, born to the Hebrews, should be killed. God protected Moses at the time for a reason. His mother kept him secret for three months, but when it was no longer possible, she took him to the riverbank because she did not want to witness how he would die.

The hand of God that was upon him made the daughter of Pharaoh see him. Taken to the palace, he became the boy of the kingdom. Unknown to Pharaoh's daughter, the divine hand of God made a way that Moses's mother was the Hebrew woman who was employed by Pharaoh's daughter to nurse him. Everyone knew him as the son of the palace, an Egyptian, but when he was growing up, his mother disclosed to him that he was an Israelite. The knowledge of this emboldened him to murder and bury in the sand an Egyptian boy who was fighting against a Hebrew boy. When Pharaoh heard this, Moses, the murderer, ran away to Midian. In all those years, Moses had never had any experience with God.

Moses's encounter with God in the miracle of the burning bush was a turning point. At the scene of the burning bush, God gave Moses the commission to go and deliver the Hebrews from the bondage of Egypt. The same Moses who had engaged in fighting and killing in his youthful exuberance was reluctantly facing the call of God. In all his years, God had been very patient with him. God had been dealing with him with prevenient grace with such a long rope to pull. Even with all his excuses, God had been dealing with him with understanding.

Moses was very reluctant to answer God's call, and one could understand why he was so reluctant. Although it had been forty years since he ran away from Pharaoh because of the homicide he committed in his youthful exuberance, the fear of facing Pharaoh was still haunting him. Even though Pharaoh he knew had died, he feared that the record of his atrocity would be known by the new pharaoh. Moreover, he had not developed faith and confidence in the Lord God sending him out. How can you rely on someone you do not know? Rationally, it would be unreasonable to walk in the night on terrain you never knew during the day.

Moses was also contemplating the people he was being asked to deliver and the Egyptians. He was envisaging that the Hebrews would not believe that God was sending him to deliver them out of the bondage of Egypt. He was also afraid that the Egyptians and the taskmasters would kill him if they discovered that he was trying to take their groaning "slaves" away:

> Who am I that I should go to Pharaoh, and that I should bring the children of Israel out of Egypt? (Ex. 3:11)

He looked at himself as being grossly inadequate. He was thinking of his incapability. He was thinking of his flaws. He was looking at his frailty. He never knew that God does not depend on humans' abilities:

> Not many wise according to the flesh, not many mighty, not many noble, are called. But God has chosen the foolish things of the world to put to shame the wise, and God has chosen the weak things of the world to put to shame the things which are mighty. (1 Cor. 1:26–27)

Like Moses, we often think that it is our ability, our wisdom, our nobility, or our might that God wants to use when He calls us. But it is the Lord God who provides for His work. God does not depend on humans' abilities. God calls, empowers, and sends us to the field:

> These signs will follow those who believe: In My name they will cast out demons; they will speak with new tongues; they will take up serpents; and

> if they drink anything deadly, it will by no means
> hurt them; they will lay hands on the sick, and they
> will recover. (Mk. 16:17–18)

In all of Moses's complaints, God was replying to him with miracles. For example, he asked, "What if they do not believe me?" God asked him what he had in his hand, and he replied, "A rod." God said, "Cast it on the ground." (Ex. 4:3). When he did, the rod became a serpent. God asked him to take it by the tail, and when he did, the serpent became a rod again. Furthermore, Moses complained that he was a stammerer and was "slow of speech" (v. 10). He asked God to send another person (v. 13). That was why God chose Aaron as Moses's assistant. But, if Moses had believed God that he would succeed, Aaron would not have come into the picture to share in the glory given to him. Unfortunately, the same Aaron was the one who contributed to the problems of Israel when he shaped the golden calf for the people of Israel to worship idols when Moses was delayed on the mount.

But there is a great lesson to learn in this dramatic call and the reluctance of Moses. It is very important to anyone who wants to engage in the Great Commission to be aware that God is the Caller, and we must be sure of and be true to our calling:

> And no man takes this honor to himself, but he
> who is called by God, just as Aaron was. (Heb. 5:4)

In a way, it was great that Moses took time to be sure that God was the One calling him—and that God was able to lead him to success. Assuming he was not called and was just dabbling in it, he would have been like Ahimaaz, who was not sent a message but outran the Cushite who was actually sent, only for Ahimaaz to find himself a failure at the end:

> Then Joab said to the Cushite, "Go, tell the king what you have seen." So the Cushite bowed himself to Joab and ran. And Ahimaaz the son of Zadok said again to Joab, "But whatever happens, please let me also run after the Cushite." So Joab said, "Why will you run, my son, since you have no news ready?" "But whatever happens," he said, "let me run." So he said to him, "Run." Then Ahimaaz ran by way of the plain, and outran the Cushite. Now David was sitting between the two gates. And the watchman went up to the roof over the gate, to the wall, lifted his eyes and looked, and there was a man, running alone. Then the watchman cried out and told the king. And the king said, "If he is alone, there is news in his mouth." And he came rapidly and drew near. Then the watchman saw another man running, and the watchman called to the gatekeeper and said, "There is another man, running alone!" And the king said, "He also brings news." So the watchman said, "I think the running of the first is like the running of Ahimaaz the son of Zadok." And the king said, "He is a good man, and comes with good news." So Ahimaaz called out and said to the king, "All is well!" Then he bowed

down with his face to the earth before the king, and said, "Blessed be the Lord your God, who has delivered up the men who raised their hand against my lord the king!" The king said, "Is the young man Absalom safe?" Ahimaaz answered, "When Joab sent the king's servant and me your servant, I saw a great tumult, but I did not know what it was about." And the king said, "Turn aside and stand here." So he turned aside and stood still. Just then the Cushite came, and the Cushite said, "There is good news, my lord the king! For the Lord has avenged you this day of all those who rose against you." And the king said to the Cushite, "Is the young man Absalom safe?" So the Cushite answered, "May the enemies of my lord the king, and all who rise against you to do harm, be like that young man!" Then the king was deeply moved, and went up to the chamber over the gate, and wept. And as he went, he said thus: "O my son Absalom—my son, my son Absalom—if only I had died in your place! O Absalom my son, my son!" (2 Samuel 18:21–33)

Absalom wanted to hijack the throne from his father, King David, because he had heard that Solomon had been appointed to step on the throne after the death of their father. For this purpose, Absalom proclaimed himself the king while the king was still alive, waged war against his father, and gathered all of Israel with himself against the warriors of David. Although David pleaded with his warriors to spare the life of his son, Absalom, he eventually died in the war. Then Joab, the captain, sent the Cushite to disclose the death of Absalom to the king. Ahimaaz, who did not know about the incident, decided to go to the king without knowing what had happened. He wanted to take pride in going to the king, but he had no message. But when the Cushite who had the message reached the king, the message made a great difference to the extent that the king wept over Absalom losing his life.

Because Moses was patient and careful to know God was sending him and received power for the mission, he was able to lead the Israelites from Egypt. He was no longer reluctant! When Moses understood the assignment God gave him, he faced it seriously. As children of God, we should not hold the work of evangelism with hands of levity. In the midst of difficulties, persecution, and intimidations, Moses never looked back.

After getting out of Egypt, the Egyptians pursued them with the intent to destroy them. Moses kept on encouraging the people, and when they got to the Red Sea, they faced a dilemma. The Red Sea was in front of them, and they could not go farther. The army of Egypt was encroaching them behind, running to catch them. On the right side was a very high and steep mountain that could not be climbed. There was another mountain on their left side. They were perplexed!

Moses was confused and frightened. The children of Israel cried out to the Lord. They yelled at Moses and complained that he should have left them in Egypt. They questioned why he had brought them out of Egypt to die in the wilderness. It would have been better for them to serve the Egyptians than to die in the wilderness.

In that kind of atmosphere, Moses demonstrated a high level of professionalism and vocational competency by persuading the people to do away with fear and see the salvation of the Lord. He assured them that the Lord would fight for them. The Egyptians would see them no more (Ex. 14:13).

Moses did not know what to do at that moment, and he cried out to God.

> Why do you cry to Me? Tell the children of Israel to go forward. But lift up your rod, and stretch out your hand over the sea and divide it. And the children of Israel shall go on dry ground through the midst of the sea. (Ex. 14:15–16)

When Moses stretched out his rod to the sea, the sea parted. The people of Israel crossed over on dry land. As soon as they crossed over, the Lord commanded Moses to stretch out the rod to the sea again, and the water returned and overtook the Egyptians. If we faithfully follow God's instructions, victory is on our side.

4.2 The Suffering of Evangelism in the Hands of Its Exponents

The early church understood the Great Commission. The apostles and the believers were witnesses.[21] On a daily basis—in houses, on streets, in villages, in marketplaces, and on roadways—they preached Christ through faith sharing by word, deeds, and signs.

---

[21] T. L. Osborn, *Soulwinning: Out Where the Sinners Are*, OSFO (1977).

They would reach "every creature" and "all nations" as rapidly as possible—in spite of deadly oppositions. They were so much in anticipation of the return of Jesus Christ. This is why they witnessed it. They knew that Christ was not dead, but He lived in them and was doing the same things He did before He was crucified. They understood that Christ could only speak and witness through them.

This passion for souls so gripped the early Christians that they spread the Gospel testimony across most of the then-known world. Down across the Mediterranean, the message went until North Africa was dotted with Christian places of worship. Passing through storms, dangers at sea, perils of ancient travel, and every other conceivable hardship, they took the message with unequaled gallantry.

The church today makes one wonder how much more time God can hold back from executing His threat to spew this Laodicean thing out of His mouth. Leonard Ravenhill said, "If there is one thing preachers agree upon, it is that this is the Laodicean age in the church."[22] We, the present church members, are lean, indolent, luxury-loving, loveless, and lacking people. Though our merciful God will pardon our sins, purge our iniquity, and pity our ignorance, our lukewarm hearts are an abomination in His sight. We must be hurt or cold, flaming or freezing, burning out or cast out. Lack of heat, lack of love, and lack of compassion for the unreached, God hates. Christ is now "wounded in the house of His friends." The Holy Book of the living God suffers more from its exponents today than from its opponents!

---

[22] L. Ravenhill, *Why Revival Tarries* (London: Send the Light Trust, 1972), 82.

God has nothing more to offer to this world. He gave His only begotten Son for sinners, He gave the Bible for all people, and He gave the Holy Spirit to convict the world and equip the church. It is now left for us to launch out, rightly dividing the word of truth. "Behold, I stand at the door and knock" (Rev. 3:20). This text has nothing to do with sinners and a waiting Savior. No! This is the tragic picture of our Lord at the door of his own Laodicean Church, trying to get in. Again, in the majority of prayer services, we often use this text from Matthew: "Where two or three are gathered together in my name, there am I in the midst of them" (Mat 18:20). But too often He is not in the midst; He is at the door! We sing His praise but shun His person!

One is not so much marveled at the patience of the Lord with the stonyhearted sinners of the day. After all, would we not be patient with a person who was both blind and deaf? And so it is with the sinners. The Lord is patient with the sleepy, sluggish, and selfish church. We, believers of today, are too slow for God's liking. We have a great responsibility that has to do with life and death upon our heads. We are bankrupt and negligent, yet we are boasters of great achievements.

In his explanation of what the church is, Solaru compares the church with the Hebrews who were special people to God. They were sent to the rest of the world to teach them His truth.[23] However, the Hebrews fell away and were not able to fulfill this mission because of their negligence and selfishness. Christ Jesus came and established a new covenant out of which a new congregation of people arose. These people—known as the New Israel—became a special people

---

[23] T. T. Solaru, *The Apostles' Creed*. Litt. Dept., MCN (1974).

unto God. This is the church, the body of believers who will fulfill the mission. The church started well, but where is it going to end?

Before Jesus Christ went to heaven, He asked a very great and thought-provoking question: "When the Son of Man comes, will He really find faith on the earth?" (Lk. 18:8[b]). For the church to remain in the faith, we must work hard and ensure that we "contend earnestly for the faith which was once for all delivered to the saints" (Jude 1:3).

In 1786, John Wesley expressed his greatest fear concerning Methodist people, his Christian fold:

> I am not afraid that the people called Methodists should ever cease to exist either in Europe or America. But I am afraid lest they should only exist as a dead sect, having the form of religion without the power. And this undoubtedly will be the case unless they hold fast both the doctrine, spirit, and discipline with which they first set out.[24]

Is this not applicable to the whole of the militant church today? We all need to think twice and be wise.

4.3 WHY EVANGELISM IS NEGLECTED

Most Christians neglect evangelism for many reasons. The following are some of the reasons why evangelism is so treated with the hands of levity:

---

[24] John Wesley. AZQuotes.com, Wind and Fly LTD, 2023.https://www. azquotes.com/quote/1316030, accessed April 23, 2023.

4.3.1 Evangelism Is Neglected Because of Ignorance

Our inexcusable ignorance has made us neglect evangelism today. In the interpretation of the parable of the sower, Jesus said, "When anyone hears the word of the kingdom, and does not understand it, then the wicked one comes and snatches away what was sown in his heart (Mat. 13:19). Because of laziness and carefree attitudes, many Christians do not want to learn or search the scriptures to acquire knowledge.

> My people are destroyed for lack of knowledge. Because you have rejected knowledge, I also will reject you from being priest for Me; Because you have forgotten the law of your God, I also will forget your children. (Hosea 4:6)

We are loose in the use of scriptural phrases, lopsided in interpreting them, and lazy to the point of impotence in appropriating their measureless wealth. No such slow-hearted, reluctant person will receive any commendation from Christ the Lord.

After His resurrection, Jesus revealed himself to the disciples who never believed He was, but he knew they were willing:

> And He opened their understanding, that they might comprehend the scriptures. (Lk 24:45)

If we are willing, the Lord is ready to open our understanding too. Nobody will take any credit for being ignorant. Every Christian should go to the Lord and say, "Lord, I am willing, open my understanding and use me. Remove ignorance from my life and teach me Your way."

4.3.2 Evangelism Is Neglected Because of Fear

As people of God who have received the Great Commission, we are quiet because of the false religions that are threatening and causing confusion as if salvation belongs to them: "There is no other name under heaven" (Acts 4:12). Only Jesus can save!

With boldness, Elijah taunted the prophets of Baal and spoke confidently about the living God. Religion without Christ does a lot of damage to the souls of people because it bars them from the true God and makes hell their final abode. Are there no children of God to spread the good news?

As recorded by Leonard Ravenhill, John Wesley fearlessly took his ground when he was intimidated by locking the doors of the English churches against him. He was not moved by the persecution he faced. Rowland Hill said, "He and laylubbers his ragged legion of preaching tinkers, scavengers, draymen, and chimney sweepers, et cetera—go forth to poison the minds of men."[25]

What a reproach of the highest order! But Wesley feared neither man nor devils. Christians were stoned and suffered every ignominy. If sin and sinners have not changed, can we preachers no longer raise the wrath of hell? Why is the work of evangelism fading away for fear of persecution and trial of faith? Christians should rise up from this lowest ebb of operation.

---

[25] L. Ravenhill, Ibid., 48.

4.3.3 Evangelism Is Neglected Because of Worldly Cares and the Deceitfulness of Riches

Many Christians are so occupied with sensual things that they do not have time for spiritual matters. Worldly cares blind their eyes to the needs of others.

In Jesus's parable of the sower, the seed that fell upon thorns "is he who hears the word, and the cares of this world and the deceitfulness of riches choke the word, and he becomes unfruitful" (Mat. 13:22). They "are those who, when they have heard, go out and are choked with cares, riches, and pleasures of life, and bring no fruit to maturity" (Lk. 8:14).

Some people prefer accumulating wealth in this transient world to spreading the Gospel for the extension of the kingdom of God. If someone sets their mind to seeking pleasure and worldly enjoyment, they will not be able to have time for caring for the salvation of others. It is where your treasure is that your mind will be.

A life of ease, delicacy, and extravagance is not an example of the life of Christ and the apostles. The uniform teaching of Jesus Christ is living a life of godliness and contentment:

> Now godliness with contentment is great gain. For we brought nothing into this world, and it is certain we can carry nothing out. And having food and clothing, with these we shall be content. But those who desire to be rich fall into temptation and a snare, and into many foolish and harmful lusts which drown men in destruction and perdition.

For the love of money is a root of all kinds of evil, for which some have strayed from the faith in their greediness, and pierced themselves through with many sorrows. But you, O man of God, flee these things and pursue righteousness, godliness, faith, love, patience, gentleness. Fight the good fight of faith, lay hold on eternal life, to which you were also called and have confessed the good confession in the presence of many witnesses. (1 Tim. 6: 6–12)

4.3.4 Evangelism Is Neglected Because of Exaggerated Doctrinal Prejudice

Peter humbly confessed, "For we did not follow cunningly devised fables when we made known to you the power and coming of our Lord Jesus Christ, but were eyewitnesses of His majesty" (2 Pet. 1:16). Peter was prominent among the disciples of Jesus Christ and moved in and out with Him during His earthly ministry. If anyone should talk about the doctrinal standard of Jesus Christ, it should be Peter.

We, in this generation, should not be denied the opportunity to hear the declaration of the truth from the apostle John:

That which was from the beginning, which we have heard, which we have seen with our eyes, which we have looked upon, and our hands have handled, concerning the Word of life— This is the message which we have heard from Him and declare to you,

that God is light and in Him is no darkness at all.
(1 John 1:1, 5)

These apostles have firsthand information, and they declare in simple terms the message of Christ. Our duty is to preach Christ and make His redemptive work prominent when we preach to sinners. This is evangelism. This is the Great Commission.

Unfortunately, many evangelists today have undue projections of their own personalities, egos, desires, and purposes. They harp on pet and favorite doctrines in Gospel presentations to sinners, which hinders its effect:

> But we have renounced the hidden things of shame, not walking in craftiness nor handling the Word of God deceitfully, but by manifestation of the truth commending ourselves to every man's conscience in the sight of God. For we do not preach ourselves, but Christ Jesus the Lord, and ourselves your bondservants for Jesus's sake. (2 Cor. 4:2, 5)

When we preach anything besides Christ, the Great Commission is compromised, which defeats the purpose of preaching. Twisting the Word of God to suit our own purpose will never bring out the purpose of God. Many prophets, founders, senior apostles, most senior apostles, et cetera—through their own self-conceited ideologies and exaggerated doctrinal prejudices—have deviated from the Great Commission instead of upholding it.

4.3.5 Evangelism Is Neglected Due to Prayerlessness, a Lack of Compassionate Love, and a Lack of Tact

Evangelism is a spiritual work that must be handled prayerfully, lovingly, and tactfully. The arm of flesh shall surely fail. No matter the strength, the zeal, the wherewithal we put into it, without the presence of the Savior to do His own part, all the labor is in vain. That is why we need to constantly get in touch with the throne above through effectual, fervent prayer.

The secret of prayer is praying in secret. Before a child is brought to life, the mother has to labor. Vital preaching and leading of souls to Christ must come out of sustained watches in the prayer chamber. Just as in atomic energy, modern scientists have touched on a new dimension of power. The church has to discover the unlimited power of the Holy Spirit through the efficacy of prayer.

Elijah was skilled in the art of prayer, and he altered the course of nature and strangled the economy of a nation. He prayed—and fire fell. He prayed—and people fell. He prayed—and rain fell. The churches are so parched that seed cannot germinate. Our altars are dry, and there are no hot tears of penitents. When Israel cried for water, Moses smote a rock, and that flinty fortress became a womb out of which a life-giving stream was born. Should we also not cry to God for these sin-ridden people in our nation to be born into the kingdom of Christ?

Moses cried out in heartbroken mourning:

> Oh, these people have committed a great sin, and
> have made for themselves a god of gold! Yet now,
> if You will forgive their sin—but if not, I pray,

blot me out of Your book which You have written.
(Exo. 32:31–32)

It took a burdened, pain-gripped Paul to say, "I have great sorrow and continual grief in my heart. For I could wish that I myself were accursed from Christ for my brethren, my countrymen according to the flesh" (Rom. 9:2–3). For this sin-hungry age, we need a prayer-hungry church. That which is born in prayer will survive the test of time.

5

THE BENEFITS OF EVANGELISM

The physical and spiritual benefits of the Gospel of faith in Jesus Christ cannot possibly be set down in human language or calculated by human mathematical minds. From the day of Pentecost, when Christ's little church in Jerusalem won three thousand persons in one day to eternal life, in obedience to Christ, up to the time of the Great Wesleyan revivals and others, through which several hundreds of thousands of people professed Christ were renewed and restored in faith to the joy of Salvation, evangelism has blessed humanity in no small measure. Many great movements for God's kingdom have been inaugurated, the course of Christ has been set forward, and the glory to His holy name have become immeasurable. The following benefits are identified through the course of history on evangelism.

5.1 Uplifting Churches and Communities Out of Lethargy and Spiritual Death

Proclamation of the good news of salvation, freedom, deliverance, and emancipation from the power of darkness has lifted churches and communities out of lethargy and spiritual death to the highest tableland of spiritual power. Those who have lost hope in life or been despondent have been quickened and strengthened by the power of Jesus Christ, and they have had their hope restored and brightened when they heard the Gospel and accepted Jesus Christ as their Lord and Savior. These people have put a new life into dead communities and aroused energies in lethargic congregations. Life has become vibrant for many people around them. As believers, we have been called to share the good news of the Gospel with the world around us. When we proclaim the message of salvation to those who are lost, we have the privilege of seeing the transformative power of the Gospel at work in the lives of individuals and in the community as a whole.

The Gospel has the power to change hearts and minds, break down walls of division, and bring healing and reconciliation where there is brokenness and pain. When we preach the Gospel, we are bringing light into darkness and hope into despair.

In the life of a community, the impact of evangelism can be truly remarkable. The Gospel is not just a message for individuals; it is a message that has the power to transform whole communities. When people come to faith in Christ, they are transformed from the inside out, and their lives are filled with a new sense of purpose and meaning. As more and more people in a community come to faith, this transformation can have a ripple effect that touches every aspect of life. Families are strengthened, relationships are restored, and communities are knit together in a bond of love and fellowship that transcends social, economic, and cultural barriers.

Evangelism can also have a positive impact on the physical and material well-being of a community. As believers are inspired to love and serve their neighbors, they become agents of change in their communities, working to alleviate poverty, promote justice, and care for the most vulnerable among us.

However, the impact of evangelism is not limited to the temporal realm. The Gospel has eternal significance; it offers the hope of salvation and eternal life to all who believe. When we share the Gospel with others, we are inviting them into a relationship with God that will last for all eternity.

5.2 Evangelism Is Fruitful in Promoting the Kingdom of God

Evangelism is fruitful in initiating new movements for God. New agencies are organized for the promotion of Christ's kingdom as they come to know the Lord. Some people found themselves coming together as a prayer band, a revival team, a campaign crew, a counseling unit, or a Bible study group, and they constitute a formidable force for the furtherance of the Gospel.

At such a gathering during the time of the early church, the Holy Spirit used to send out groups of people for special duties:

> As they ministered to the Lord and fasted, the Holy
> Spirit said, "Now separate to Me Barnabas and Saul

for the work to which I have called them." Then,
having fasted and prayed, and laid hands on them,
they sent them away. (Acts 13:2–3)

It is marvelous and wonderful to note how mightily this team was used for the extension of God's kingdom. Going through the first, second, and third missionary journeys of Paul—as recorded in the Acts of the Apostles—one would be thrilled at the huge success he made in promoting the kingdom of God. Down through the ages, educational institutions and benevolent enterprises have found their inspiration and beginnings when the kingdom of God was extended to people through the work of evangelism.

5.3 Evangelism Transfers People from the Kingdom of Darkness to the Kingdom of Christ

The majority of people who are today—or have been in the past— disciples of Christ were won to Christ through the spreading of the Gospel. Millions of souls now in heaven and those on earth serving Christ would have been in hell—or on their way there—if the good news was not proclaimed to them at the appropriate time in their lives.

In his letter to the Colossians, Paul said, "He (God) has delivered us from the power of darkness and conveyed us into the kingdom of the Son of His love, in whom we have redemption through His blood, the forgiveness of sins" (Col. 1:13–14). There is no way this provision that is available in Jesus Christ for the whole world can be made known without proper and effective evangelism.

That was why Paul was exhorting his son in the Lord, Timothy, to "Preach the word! Be ready in season and out of season. Convince, rebuke, exhort, with all longsuffering and teaching" (2 Tim. 4:2).

As the Gospel is proclaimed, minding this exhortation, it leads to deliverance of people from sin, Satan, and the power of darkness. Osunlana stated that if anybody who has been under the rulership of the devil because of his sinful nature and love for sin, love for this present evil world and flesh, now repents and accepts Jesus as his Lord and Savior, the person shall be "translated" into the kingdom of Christ where everything will be put under their feet, including the devil, his former ruler and governor.[26] This is true and scriptural, and it is the testimony of hundreds of thousands of people who truly gave their lives to Christ. When people benefit from this Great Commission, their lives are no longer in darkness, in the hands of the devil, or in his kingdom. A miracle of transformation has taken place, and they are now in the light, in the kingdom of Christ, and in the haven of rest.

5.4 Evangelism Makes People Render Fruitful Service to God

The fountains of liberality in the hearts and purses of people are opened by evangelism. Visions of Christ's kingdom and the values of life, talents, and money put into the course of Christ have been

---

[26] S. K. Osunlana, *Faith and Miracle* (Ibadan: Feyisetan Press, 1998), 23.

found possible by the work of the Holy Spirit and the lives of those who have been evangelized.

Because of the joy of what God has wrought through Christ in their lives, people easily commit themselves to the service of the Lord. What Paul had on the Damascus Road was not an experiment; it was an experience. He had an encounter with Jesus Christ. The man who was persecuting the church had a great transformation and turned to building an empire for Christ with his colossal intellect and wonderful pedigree: "I can do all things through Christ who strengthens me" (Phil 4:13). He spent—and was spent—for the expansion of the kingdom (2 Cor. 12:15).

According to Bamgboye, evangelism is the primary duty of Christians.[27] We are saved to serve in order to save others too. As we render our services to God, more souls are won to Christ, and so we become fruitful. Those who neglect evangelism are stagnant and will be recording retrogression in their spiritual graph. If a Christian is not involved in evangelism, the person is sleeping on duty. Akinbode describes spiritual sleep as a dangerous enemy.[28] In order to set in motion what the Holy Spirit has wrought in our lives through evangelism, we must continue to make it spread to others.

5.5 Evangelism Is a Strong Apparatus for Church Expansion

Bamgboye explains that a church that evangelizes prospers (expands, develops, and progresses) and a stagnant one retrogresses

---

[27] J. A. Bamgboye, "Basic Principles of Christian Faith."

[28] G. O. Akinbode, *Marvelous in Our Eyes* (Ibadan: Feyisetan Press, 1998), 31.

(diminishes and crumbles). The kingdom of Christ is extended, but Satan is destroyed as one evangelizes. Most churches in homelands and foreign fields are started as a result of seasoned Gospel promotions.

The Cecil Williamson Ministry Council, comprising thirty laypersons and clergy members and their spouses had its focus on reviving congregations in the United States of America and establishing churches across the world, helping to facilitate the work through evangelistic campaigns abroad and revivals in the United States of America.[29] This ministry has traveled to many countries and has made a lot of impact in helping churches develop. Among the countries that benefited from this Gospel move are South Africa, the Philippines, India and the "Tata" Seamounts, Chile with Bertist Rouse and Andrew Gallman, Brazil with Rick Bonfim, Paraguay with Ben Covington, Nigeria with the Methodist Church, Nigeria, and Russia with Chris Hema and Joe Holland.

In Nigeria, the Cecil Williamson Ministry has helped churches expand remarkably. Since 1985, the team has been working with the head of the church and others such as the Methodist Evangelical Movement leaders. The ministry has been working hand in hand with the Methodist Evangelical Movement, and many lay evangelists were trained and used for church planting. No fewer than eleven new churches—with a total membership of more than three thousand new Christians—were planted during this outreach. The churches also enjoyed the provision of campaign equipment from the ministry. This access of the ministry has

---

[29] C. Williamson, "Good News Article: You can make a difference, delivered at the Methodist Ministers' Conference, Sagamu" (unpublished) (1999).

revealed how effective evangelism can lead to great improvements in the church. When members of the body of Christ move out for evangelism, retreats, revival promotions, and testimonies of success usually follow because the Lord of the work has promised to back it up.

Akinbode recorded a testimony of Sunday Moleye, a boy who could neither hear nor speak.[30] The boy spoke and heard voices for the first time during the December retreat in 1987. At the same time, two other people suffering from rheumatism and malaria fever, respectively, were healed by the power of the Lord Jesus Christ. Miracles like these are "crowd pullers" in the evangelistic outreach, and when they hear the Gospel and give their lives to Christ, the church will surely expand—and the kingdom of God will be more populated.

5.6 EVANGELISM MOVES WITH POWER AND AUTHORITY TO SAVE, HEAL, AND DELIVER

When Jesus Christ came, He fulfilled the prophecy in Isaiah 61, which He read in the presence of the people in the synagogue at Nazareth:

> The Spirit of the Lord is upon Me,
> Because He has anointed Me
> To preach the Gospel to the poor;
> He has sent Me to heal the brokenhearted,

---

[30] G. O. Akinbode, *God at Work: A Short History of the Fellowship of Evangelical Groups in the Western Part of MCN* (Ibadan: Scripture Union Press, 1992).

To proclaim liberty to the captives
And recovery of sight to the blind,
To set at liberty those who are oppressed;
To proclaim the acceptable year of the Lord. (Lk.
4:18–19)

In other words, Jesus was saying, "I have seen your troubles, and I have come to deliver you." He specializes in difficult cases. Only Jesus Christ can cure the diseases that are incurable to humans, including the influence of the devil. We need to seek the power of Jesus Christ because of the condition of the world. Something terrible has befallen the earth. A voice spoke from heaven:

> Therefore rejoice, O heavens, and you who dwell in them! Woe to the inhabitants of the earth and the sea! For the devil has come down to you, having great wrath, because he knows that he has a short time. (Rev. 12:12)

The earth is in trouble because the devil has been cast down from heaven. That is why all kinds of plagues are in the world. That is why we hear about incurable diseases. Evil spirits have filled the land, air, and sea. The earth is in trouble! Everywhere is polluted with diseases, calamities, plagues, cancer, hypertension, pneumonia, yellow fever, migraines, tuberculosis, heart disease, meningitis, cholera, stroke, Ebola, flu, diarrhea, HIV/AIDS, chronic obstructive pulmonary disease, and more.

The devil is selling all kinds of diseases to people. A heart attack is two dollars. A stomach pain is one dollar. A stroke is one dollar. If you buy a disease from the devil for one dollar, you cannot sell it back for the same price. You could spend thousands of dollars on it, but you will still be troubled. People are inflicted with blindness, dumbness, lameness, hemorrhages, barrenness, weakness, sleeplessness, unrest, and drunkenness. That is why Jesus declares in John 10:10, "The thief does not come except to steal, and to kill, and to destroy. I have come that they may have life, and that they may have it more abundantly."

Why do we need Jesus? Christ, our Master, has released the power of signs and wonders to us. He gave us the power—without measure—because He had gone to the Father. What did Jesus do? He healed the sick, raised the dead, delivered the oppressed, cast out demons, cleansed the lepers, and preached the Gospel of the kingdom. All these things were done for us. We must use the authority He has bestowed on us:

> Most assuredly, I say to you, he who believes in Me, the works that I do he will do also; and greater works than these he will do, because I go to My Father. (Jn. 14:12)

As we obey the call to evangelize, we will minister with the power and authority given by the Holy Spirit to heal the sick, set the captives free from bondage, and minister salvation to them. The Lord Jesus Christ started with the twelve disciples. He saw the suffering of the people. He saw how the devil was tormenting the people. He saw many who were inflicted with illnesses, disease, and pestilence. He saw how many were languishing in sin and in total darkness.

> Then He called His twelve disciples together and
> gave them power and authority over all demons,
> and to cure diseases. He sent them to preach the
> kingdom of God and to heal the sick. (Lk. 9:1–2)

The Lord does not leave the work to us alone. He goes with us with signs and wonders manifesting as we evangelize. We could see this evidence when He sent out the disciples:

> After these things the Lord appointed seventy
> others also and sent them two by two before His
> face into every city and place where He Himself
> was about to go. Then He said to them, "The
> harvest truly is great, but the laborers are few;
> therefore pray the Lord of the harvest to send out
> laborers into His harvest." (Lk. 10:1–2)

It is exciting to note the testimony of the disciples when they returned and the response of Jesus Christ:

> Then the seventy returned with joy, saying, "Lord,
> even the demons are subject to us in Your name."
> And He said to them, "I saw Satan fall like lightning
> from heaven. Behold, I give you the authority to
> trample on serpents and scorpions, and over all the
> power of the enemy, and nothing shall by any means
> hurt you. Nevertheless do not rejoice in this, that the
> spirits are subject to you, but rather rejoice because
> your names are written in heaven." (Lk. 10:17–20)

> All authority has been given to Me in heaven and
> on earth. (Mat. 28)

After He had done everything, He gave it to the church. However, Jesus did not give His garment to His church. When we observe what He gave to the church, it was not His shoes, His sandals, or His mantle. It was not candles or oil. One of the great things He left for us is power. No believer—no child of God— should stay without power. All believers must carry this power:

> Behold, I give you the authority to trample on
> serpents and scorpions, and over all the power of
> the enemy, and nothing shall by any means hurt
> you. (Lk. 10:19)

It is wonderful to know the One who has all power and finds nothing impossible. The person who has received Christ into their life has received the One who is the source and possessor of all power. His power will work for you, in you, and through you:

> And these signs will follow those who believe: In
> My name they will cast out demons; they will speak
> with new tongues; they will take up serpents; and
> if they drink anything deadly, it will by no means
> hurt them; they will lay hands on the sick, and they
> will recover. (Mk. 16:17–18)

Jesus has the power to control all things because He created all things:

For by Him all things were created that are in heaven and that are on earth, visible and invisible, whether thrones or dominions or principalities or powers. All things were created through Him and for Him. (Col. 1:16)

The power of Jesus surpasses the knowledge of the Pharisees and teachers:

Now it happened on a certain day, as He was teaching, that there were Pharisees and teachers of the law sitting by, who had come out of every town of Galilee, Judea, and Jerusalem. And the power of the Lord was present to heal them. (Lk. 5:17)

It is one thing to get an education and study law or philosophy, but it is another thing to have the power of God. The Pharisees and doctors were very prominent in society, but they still had problems they could not solve. They came from Galilee, Judea, and Jerusalem to be healed. Many spiritual problems cannot be solved by education:

With men, this is impossible, but with God all things are possible. (Mt. 19:26)

You cannot read a book to get this! You cannot acquire a certificate to get this. You cannot buy this in a mall. You cannot use formulas for this! The Pythagorean theory and mathematical formulas cannot give you this power. You can only receive this power from Christ.

Simon was a sorcerer who wanted to buy God's power. He had been practicing sorcery in Samaria to show people his power. He deceived the people for a long time, and they thought he possessed the power of God—until Philip visited Samaria with the Gospel. All the people believed Philip as he preached the things about the kingdom of God and the name of Jesus Christ. Many men and women were baptized, including Simon the sorcerer. When Simon was baptized, he was amazed to see the miracles and signs that Philip performed. Peter and John joined Philip in Samaria, and when they laid hands on the people, they were baptized with the Holy Spirit.

When Simon saw that the Holy Spirit was given via laying on of the apostles' hands, he offered them money. He wanted the power to lay hands on people and give them the Holy Spirit. Peter, moved by the Holy Spirit, rebuked him:

> Your money perish with you, because you thought that the gift of God could be purchased with money! You have neither part nor portion in this matter, for your heart is not right in the sight of God. (Acts 8:18–21)

The power to heal and do miracles belongs to God and manifests in the lives of God's children. Paul said, "I can do all things through Christ who strengthens me" (Phil. 4:13).

Generally, the Bible speaks of two kinds of power. God offers both to Christians who engage in the work of evangelism. One is the dynamic power (Greek: *dunamis*) of ability, energy, and strength. The other is the legal power (Greek: *exousia*) of authority, right, dominion, and attorney. Jesus gave His disciples "power (*dunamis*) and authority (*exousia*) over all devils and to cure diseases" (Lk 9:1; 10:19–21). No sickness can stand before the mighty Spirit of God. Your body is His temple. If you allow Him, He will keep His temple free from sin, sickness, and satanic attacks.

When I was serving at Immanuel-First Spanish United Methodist Church in Brooklyn, I experienced the mighty hand of God. One of the church members was sick and in the hospital. After the service on Sunday, I went to visit her. When I got there, I saw many people in the ward. I could sense their sorrow. I moved near her bed, and I said, "Let us pray."

As I was praying, the woman coughed, opened her eyes, and whispered, "Pastor, thank you."

The whole place was filled with shouts of joy. Her husband held me and said, "Thank you, Pastor."

I did not know that the woman had already been declared dead. One of her daughters was on the phone when I entered, and she had already phoned her sister in Pennsylvania to say that their mother had passed. She quickly called again to say she had come back to life.

The woman was released from the hospital on the third day.

Nothing is too hard for God! By the time I was appointed to another church, according to the bishop's schedule, the husband of the woman was begging them not to remove me from the church. The schedule had already been finalized. I made it known, however, that the Lord is the one who is doing the miracles—and He can use anyone to fulfill His purpose.

When I was serving at Cuyler-Warren Street United Methodist Church, one of the members of the church came with his friend one day. The man was about thirty-five years old. He had been unable to sleep for the ten days. I asked him to explain what he had been doing before he started experiencing the problem. He was very poor and could hardly maintain his life. He often had difficulty getting food, clothing, and accommodation. As a result, he was looking for a way to become rich. He had been introduced to a man who made a concoction for him. He would lick it in the morning and at night before going to bed. He kept a small object made of animal skin in his wallet at all times. Since he had acquired those things, he had been hearing scary voices at night and was always filled with fear.

I counseled him and introduced Jesus to him. I explained that he had subjected himself to the spirit world. Jesus is the only One who can deliver a person from the power of darkness, and the man needed to accept Jesus Christ as his Lord and Savior.

He agreed.

I led him to a prayer of confession, request for forgiveness, and acceptance of Jesus Christ as his personal Lord and Savior. I asked if he could release the materials he was using.

He went and got the concoction and the talisman.

We prayed and destroyed them and their effects upon him in the name of Jesus Christ.

The man testified later that he had been sleeping well—and God had been helping him. Christ's power is available to save, heal, and deliver!

The risen Savior did not give us a powerless Great Commission. The Gospel goes out with power and authority. Jesus made a promise to us:

> You shall receive power when the Holy Spirit has
> come upon you; and you shall be witnesses to Me
> in Jerusalem, and in all Judea and Samaria, and to
> the end of the earth. (Acts 1:8)

Peter denied Jesus in front of a small girl because of his fear. When Jesus was arrested, Peter was hiding from the soldiers. He was filled with the Holy Spirit and became powerful.

> Peter, standing up with the eleven, raised his voice
> and said to them, "Men of Judea and all who dwell
> in Jerusalem, let this be known to you, and heed my
> words" ... Therefore let all the house of Israel know
> assuredly that God has made this Jesus, whom you
> crucified, both Lord and Christ. (Acts 2:14, 36)

The power of God touched many souls, and they asked what they would do. Then Peter declared to them, "Repent, and let every one of you be baptized in the name of Jesus Christ for the remission of sins; and you shall receive the gift of the Holy Spirit" (Acts 2:14; Acts 2:36–38). He spoke with power and authority. He raised his voice with confidence and fervor and said, "Repent and be baptized." That is the Gospel. Christ sets free! That is the Gospel! Jesus Christ can never lose His power. Christ is the same yesterday, today, and forever, and He has given us the power to spread the good news.

After the resurrection of our Lord, He gave the Great Commission to His followers, which became the pattern of their lives. This is what has been passed on until it came to us. The Great

Commission came with power, doctrine, and a way of life. Those who want to be empowered in the Gospel must follow the way of life and the pattern that Jesus laid down for the apostles:

> And they continued steadfastly in the apostles' doctrine and fellowship, in the breaking of bread, and in prayers. Then fear came upon every soul, and many wonders and signs were done through the apostles. (Acts 2:42–43)

They continued steadfastly in the apostles' doctrine. That was the pattern of their lives. They continued steadfastly in fellowship. That was the pattern of their lives. They continued steadfastly in the breaking of bread. That was the pattern of their lives. They continued steadfastly in prayer. That was the pattern of their lives.

> Now all who believed were together, and had all things in common, and sold their possessions and goods, and divided them among all, as anyone had need. So continuing daily with one accord in the temple, and breaking bread from house to house, they ate their food with gladness and simplicity of heart, praising God and having favor with all the people. And the Lord added to the church daily those who were being saved. (Acts 2:44–47)

This scripture reminds me of our group at the Methodist Evangelical Movement (MEM) in Nigeria. Seven like-minded youths in our church, Methodist Church, Agodi Ibadan, decided to gather on Wednesdays to pray and study the Word of God together. We started in a small way, but we were increasing rapidly. We saw ourselves as brothers and sisters and were so united in Christ that we were helping each another physically and spiritually. We were desperate to spread the Gospel!

Within a short time, we had spread our fellowship to several churches in Ibadan and other towns and villages. Amazingly, our group was accepted in all the Methodist churches in Nigeria, and we had a Department of Evangelism at the apex of the Methodist Church in Nigeria. Many churches were planted by MEM, and the work of church planting still continues today. It has been my earnest prayer that the good work that the Lord started will continue to flourish.

The church today needs to be careful about false doctrine and false teachers. As the work of God was expanding in the hands of the early disciples, a seed of false doctrine was sown by certain false teachers, causing some to waver in their faith regarding the Second Coming of Christ. That prompted Paul to narrate the events that must take place first. Some of the believers were deceived, thinking that Christ's coming was very near, and they gave up their jobs and became idle. Defending the events of the Lord's coming and other doctrines of the apostles, Paul wrote a letter to the Thessalonian Christians:

> Not to be soon shaken in mind or troubled, either
> by spirit or by word or by letter, as if from us, as
> though the day of Christ had come. Let no one
> deceive you by any means; for that Day will not

come unless the falling away comes first, and the
man of sin is revealed, the son of perdition. (2
Thess. 2:2–3)

In this context, we carefully follow the traditions of the early
disciples. The word *tradition* is used in several ways in the New
Testament. It means handing down or handing over for the purpose
of onward transmission to the coming generation. The second
way the word *tradition* is used is to refer to apostolic teaching,
ordinances, and doctrine of the Christian faith: the Holy Spirit-
given doctrine. Paul warned the Thessalonian Christians:

> Therefore, brethren, stand fast and hold the
> traditions which you were taught, whether by word
> or our epistle. (2 Thess. 2:15)

> Moreover, brethren, I declare to you the Gospel
> which I preached to you, which also you received
> and in which you stand, by which also you are
> saved, if you hold fast that word which I preached to
> you—unless you believed in vain. (1 Cor. 15:1–2)

> But we command you, brethren, in the name of our
> Lord Jesus Christ, that you withdraw from every
> brother who walks disorderly and not according to
> the tradition which he received from us (2 Thess. 3:6)

We are not to keep human traditions that contradict the
inspired, inerrant, and infallible Word of God. We are not to keep

any ecclesiastical pronouncement of uninspired human-made traditions. Paul, inspired by the Holy Spirit, revealed the traditions to keep: "Keep the traditions. Don't change the traditions" (Gal 1:7–9).

Hold fast to the sound doctrine of the apostles, which was given to them by Jesus Christ. We are to continue steadfastly in the apostles' doctrine, on faith in God, Jesus Christ, the Holy Spirit, repentance and forgiveness, salvation by grace, new birth, sanctification, love, holiness, water baptism, Holy Spirit baptism, holy matrimony, a Spirit-controlled domestic life, and a decent public life.

Paul instructed Titus to charge them in Ephesus and teach no other doctrine besides the apostolic traditions (1 Tim 1:3). Abiding in the doctrine of Christ, as taught by the apostles, is an indicator that we are in God and in Christ:

> Whoever transgresses and does not abide in the doctrine of Christ does not have God. He who abides in the doctrine of Christ has both the Father and the Son. If anyone comes to you and does not bring this doctrine, do not receive him into your house nor greet him. (2 John 9–10)

The last book of the Bible warns us not to add to or remove anything from the apostolic traditions:

> For I testify to everyone who hears the words of the prophecy of this book: If anyone adds to these things, God will add to him the plagues that are

written in this book; and if anyone takes away from the words of the book of this prophecy, God shall take away his part from the Book of Life, from the holy city, and from the things which are written in this book. (Rev. 22:18–19)

When we follow the truth, the power of God will manifest— and the Gospel of Jesus Christ will flow freely and meet the needs of the people of the world.

CONCLUSION

A Declaration of the Gospel

This is one of the most neglected commandments in God's Word. The apostles declared and testified to what they saw, heard, and knew of Jesus Christ, our Lord and Savior. It is the responsibility of all who have received salvation and any benefits of the atonement in Christ to declare to others what they have heard, seen, and learned.

The Gospel has been declared at different periods in history. At different periods and in different generations of humanity, there have always been faithful witnesses who declare God's goodness and love to others. This is our generation, and this is our chance.

The Gospel must be declared to different sections of the community. Our declaration of the Gospel must be planned to reach the poor, the rich, the captives and prisoners, women and men, the sick, children, kings and great people, religious and idolatrous people, nominal Christians and churchgoers, philosophers and intellectuals, travelers, and villagers and city dwellers. We must reach all people with the Gospel if we are to be pure from the blood of all people.

What, then, are we to declare? Many Christians who know their responsibility to "preach the Gospel" or to "declare the Truth" do not understand what to declare and how they are to go about it. We are to, in the first case, declare, "That which was from the beginning," Christ, the Savior (1 Jn. 1:1; Jn. 1:1). We are to preach Christ, clearly showing that "He died for our sins" and was "raised for our justification" (1 Cor. 15:1–4; Rom. 10:9, 10).

Second, we are to declare the message we have heard of Him (1 Jn. 1:1, 3, 5; Heb. 2:3; Mat. 28:19, 20; 2 Tim. 2:2). We cannot preach a "new revelation" that we have not heard or read in the Word of God because that would ruin our souls and send our hearers into perdition. Preaching the Word is timely and necessary today.

Third, we are to declare, "That which we have seen with our eyes" (1 Jn. 1:1–3; Mk. 5:18–20; Acts 4:20; 22:15; 26:16). If we have experienced God's salvation and have seen His saving grace, healing power, and love in our lives and in others, we cannot be quiet. We must speak out. We must testify, witness, and preach.

It is every believer's responsibility to witness, testify, and declare the Gospel. Neglect brings guilt and judgment:

> Therefore, to him who knows to do good and does
> not do it, to him it is sin. (James 4:17)

Time Is Short

The twenty-first century has put the human race on trial for its life. The issue has been human survival and salvation or obliteration. Time is short! Time is really running out. The magnetic time of the Rapture is around the corner. The church is on trial for its life. Can the church believe and work for salvation for all before Christ arrives? That is the vision of the church. It is a vision for the revival of the church and evangelization of the world.

What it takes for evil to prevail is for God's people to do nothing. This is the time to prepare in personal inner holiness, separate from the corrupt worldly system, and preach the Gospel. I want to share a message about the brevity of life and the urgency of our mission here on earth. The Bible teaches us that our time on this earth is short, and we must make the most of it.

Furthermore, James says, "Whereas you do not know what will happen tomorrow. For what is your life? It is even a vapor that appears for a little time and then vanishes away" (James 4:14). This passage underscores the fact that our lives are short and uncertain. We must, therefore, be intentional about how we spend our time.

As Christians, we have a specific mission while we are on this earth. We are called to love God with all our hearts, souls, minds, and strength and to love our neighbors as ourselves. We are also called to make disciples of all nations, baptizing them in the name of the Father, the Son, and the Holy Spirit:

> All authority has been given to Me in heaven and on earth. Go therefore and make disciples of all the nations, baptizing them in the name of the Father and of the Son and of the Holy Spirit, teaching them to observe all things that I have commanded you; and lo, I am with you always, even to the end of the age. (Mat. 28:18–20)

This passage reminds us of the urgency of our mission. We must not waste time on trivial pursuits or things that do not matter in light of eternity. Instead, we must focus on fulfilling the Great Commission and spreading the Gospel to all people.

Let us not be complacent with the time we have been given. Let us use it wisely and with purpose and intentionality. Let us love God and our neighbors, make disciples, and spread the Gospel to all who will hear. Our time on this earth is short, but our impact for the kingdom of God can be eternal. May we use the time we have been given to make a difference in this world and bring glory to God.

BIBLIOGRAPHY

Abraham, W. J. *The Logic of Evangelism*. Great Britain: Hodder and Stoughton, 1991.

Akinbode, G. O. *God at Work: A Short History of the Fellowship of Evangelical Groups in the Western Part of MCN*. Ibadan: Scripture Union Press, 1992.

Akinbode, G. O. *Marvelous in Our Eyes* Ibadan: Feyisetan Press, 1998.

Baptism, Eucharist, and Ministry. Faith and Order Paper No. 111 Geneva: World Council of Churches, 1982.

Bowen, Roger "So I Send You: A Study Guide to Mission." SPCK, *International Study Guide 34*.

Cetuk, Virginia Samuel. *What to Expect in Seminary: Theological Education as Spiritual Formation*. Nashville: Abingdon Press, 1998.

Elkins, Heather Murray. *Worshiping Women: Re-Forming God's People for Praise*. Nashville: Abingdon Press, 1994.

Fox, E. and G. Morris, *Faith-sharing: Dynamic Christian Witnessing by Invitation*, 1996.

John Wesley. AZQuotes.com, Wind and Fly LTD, 2023. https://www.azquotes.com/quote/1316030, accessed April 23, 2023.

Krass, A. C. Applied Theology 1 "Go and Make Disciples" in *Association with the United Society for Christian Litt. For the Theological Education Fund, London* SPCK, 1974.

McGrath, Alister E. *Christian Theology: An Introduction*, third ed. Malden: Blackwell Publishing, 2001.

Osborn, T. L. *Soulwinning Out Where the Sinners Are*. OSFO, USA, 1977.

Osunlana, S. K. *Faith and Miracle* Ibadan: Feyisetan Press, 1998.

Ravenhill, L. *Why Revival Tarries*. London: The Light Trust, 1972.

Schellman, James M. "Initiation: Forming Disciples for Christ's Mission in the World," in *Liturgy and Justice: To Worship God in Spirit and Truth*, ed. Anne Y. Koester Minnesota: The Liturgical Press, 2002.

Solaru, T. T. *The Apostles' Creed*. Litt. Dept., MCN, 1974.

Stott, J. *The Lausanne Covenant. Exposition and Commentary,* Minneapolis: World Wide Publication, 1975.

Printed in the United States
by Baker & Taylor Publisher Services